The Naked Accountant Asks:

Who's Standing On Your Financial Hose?

A Simple Guide to Financial Healing

jean backus, cpa, cfp

W
A PRESS
Austin, TX

Dedicated to...

My hero and husband, Andrew Backus who always believed I had a message and without whom I'd be a complete wreck;

My great friends, colleagues and spiritual advisers, Liliane and Gilles Desjardins, who never gave up on me, treated me with the brilliant Desjardins Unified Model[1] of which I use only the Ego/Identity portion in this book as well as my own life and without whom there would be no sane "me" to write the book;

My writing coach, Dr. Todd Michael, who helped clarify my message and without whom there would be no book;

and,

The Wizard Academy, who helped solidify my message and laid out the yellow brick road!

THANK YOU!!

Copyright © 2008 by Jean Backus and Wizard Academy Press. All rights reserved.

Permission to reproduce or transmit in any form or by any means, electronic or mechanical, including photocopying and recording, or by an information storage and retrieval system, must be obtained by writing to the publisher at the address below:

Wizard Academy Press
16221 Crystal Hills Drive
Austin, TX 78737
512.295.5700 voice, 512.295.5701 fax
www.WizardAcademyPress.com

Ordering Information
To order additional copies, contact your local bookstore, visit www.WizardAcademyPress.com, or call 1.800.425.4769
Quantity discounts are available.

ISBN 978-1-932226-70-6 soft cover

Library of Congress Cataloging-in-Publication Data

Backus, Jean.
     The naked accountant asks: who's standing on your financal hose. /Jean Backus.
        p.   cm.
     ISBN: 9781932226706

2009922293

First printing: November 2008
Second printing: February 2009
Third printing: August 2009
Fourth Printing: May 2010

TABLE OF CONTENTS

PREFACE — 19

Introducing the Steps
to Financial Freedom — 29
- Desjardins Ego/Identity Unified Model
- True Story #1
- True Story #2
- Prosperity Cycle

Step One – Wake Up! — 54

Step Two – Starting Point — 66

Step Three – Know The Destination — 71

Step Four – Creating The Time Line — 81

Step Five – The Plan (KISSS) — 90

Step Six – Mastering Self Talk — 95
- Poverty Cycle

Step Seven – Discipline — 108

Step Eight – Conscious Spending — 112

Step Nine – Reward Yourself — 116

Step Ten – Review The Plan — 125

Bibliography/References — 131

NOTE TO BOOK WRITTEN 3/27/10

I am excited my book is going into its Fourth Printing. I have sold some books and it is always a thrill to see a royalty check in my mailbox. However, the most exciting part of the Fourth Printing is where first three printings ended up.

I never wrote this book to become famous or make tons of money. I wrote this book because I had a story that resulted in what felt like a calling. Many people have asked, "So, where was your book signing?" or "How many copies have you sold?" etc." I did not have a book signing – never gave it much thought. Here's what I did: I put a sticker on the front of the book that said, "FINDERS KEEPERS" and a sticker inside that said, "READ, PROSPER, PASS ON". I stamped my blog, 'TheNakedAccountant.com' on a two dollar bill that served as the books' official bookmark. I would then sign the book & every time Andrew and I would travel, I would take a dozen or so copies and leave them in airports, on the plane, in the hotel and at various other locations that would strike my fancy.

In all, I have given away over 1,000 books all over the world. Whenever my friends go on a trip, I ask them if they can take a book or two and give them away. I am humbled when they graciously agree. There are now books that have made their way to France, Italy, Greece, China, Canada, Israel, Dominican Republic, Turkey, Germany, Buenos Aires, London, Wales, Scotland, Antarctic, etc. as well as much of our United States.

I'm not sure why I did this. I didn't have a grand plan. It just unfolded the way it unfolded. The best I can come up with is that I do have a message. My message is that no matter what it looks like at the moment or on the surface – it is never about the money. I think I had to demonstrate it – practice what I preach – put my money where my mouth is, so to speak.

I continue to give books away. I gave a few away today. I am writing this on a plane from Raleigh, NC to Austin, TX and I have one more book with me that I am going to leave on this plane when we touch down. I just attended a four-day intense (what I coined), 'Transplant Boot Camp' with my twin sister because she is a candidate for a liver transplant. We met with over 10 docs over a four day period and most of them got a copy of the book. So I am now going to add this dedication: "To my courageous twin, Janet Griffin & anyone else out there in the world awaiting an organ transplant."

I trust every book ends up in the perfect hands. Even if the original person does not read it, I hope they pass it on to someone who may benefit. I trust everything happens for a reason (a saying I learned from my soul sister, Debbie….).

Dr. Grant says the opposite of depression is gratitude. I do a gratitude list every morning. I am not depressed.

I believe in the power of LOVE. If you do too, read on!

INTRODUCTION
The Money Magnet
By Dr. Todd Michael

For years now, there has been a legend floating around in the New Thought zeitgeist--or mindset, if you will, of the so-called "money magnet." A money magnet is a person who supposedly has the mysterious but consistent ability to attract money. According to the lore, such a person accomplishes this attraction automatically, whether they are thinking about it or not, with no more effort, seemingly, than a metal magnet attracts iron filings. But most importantly, a money magnet is alleged to be able to magnetize other people who come in contact with them, so that they too may experience a miraculous influx of monetary resources.

The question is: "Do money magnets really exist?" I will not answer this question directly, for it is a question that every seeker on the path needs to answer for herself. But I will say this: Knowing what I now know, if I were you, I would pay close attention to the story that I am going to tell you. Because it is about a real-life money magnet, named Jean Carpenter-Backus, who will reveal the secrets to financial success that she teaches, in the book that follows. As the great divine intelligence that runs this show would have it, the privilege and responsibility to introduce this woman to you has fallen upon me.

And who am I? My name is Todd Michael. You might know me from my books, including The Evolution Angel, The Twelve Conditions of a Miracle, or The Hidden Parables which are in many foreign languages by now. Or perhaps you've heard me speak on the Art Bell Show, the Uri Geller Show from London, or at any of dozens of Unity and other New Thought Churches, book stores, and learning centers around the country.

I am a physician by training, twenty years of emergency and trauma primarily, but became an author seventeen years ago--because I found the wholly left-brained approach of Western medicine left me yearning for something more, for myself and my family. Although decent enough at both medicine and writing, I was nonetheless somewhat of an idiot when it came to money. That is, until I met Jean. I want to take a few pages to tell you the circumstances which led to my meeting this special teacher, because our meeting marked the single greatest inflection point I have ever experienced in my financial evolution.

About two months before I met her, I was speaking on the island of Maui, Hawaii, about The Hidden Parables, the last book I published and my masterpiece. At that time, I was undergoing great financial stress and I couldn't understand why. It certainly wasn't because I was not working hard enough. Maybe you can relate, because when it comes right down to it, I have been pretty much like you and a lot of other people. I was actually working my tail off but wasn't getting ahead at all. In fact, like you and a lot of other people that experience apparent financial lack, I was barely able to make ends meet. I was so discouraged at that point in time that I was contemplating giving up my entire writing career and falling back into the depressive environment of pure medicine. I needed help, and bad.

Because of this, I decided to pay homage to one of my greatest influences, Ram Dass, who lives on Maui. He had me over to his house one afternoon, and I remember thinking on the drive over that I wasn't going to ask this great man anything, this time. I had before and had miraculous answers, but things were different now. He'd had a pretty serious stroke, for God's sake, and I felt resolutely that the most appropriate thing for me to do was to visit him with the sole intention of giving him energy, not taking anything away, not bothering him with any serious questions or problems.

My partner at that time, Judy, and I sat in the spacious living room that overlooked the bluer than blue oceanscape Maui is so famous for, when he rolled himself quietly into the room in his wheelchair. Actually, he looked great, his eyes shining with happiness and wisdom and compassion as they always had. We talked for a while, until there was an unexpected lull in the conversation. I couldn't help myself somehow and it just sort of popped out of my mouth.

"Hit me with your best shot," I said to him. "Where am I weakest in my spiritual growth and my work as a teacher?" This is something spiritual teachers have to ask one another from time to time in order to keep on the straight and narrow.

I was a more than a trifle nervous about asking him this. There was no telling what kind of unsettling and confrontational response I might expect. It could even evoke a major growth crisis, as though I needed another one to deal with at the time. Perhaps he would say something about my ego getting too big about this or about being lazy about that. His response was completely unexpected: He said absolutely nothing, closing his eyes and falling into a state of meditation for about three or four minutes.

Now, that might not sound like that long to you, but sitting there in this great man's house, steeling myself to hear about my deepest and most shameful shortcomings as a teacher, it seemed like an eternity. Finally, he opened his giant, shining Einsteinian eyes and rolled his chair up close in front of me and looked directly into my eyes.

"Your angels are real," he said.

It hit me like a ton of bricks. Now, how on earth could he have possibly known that I was a) working with angels or b) experiencing intense doubts about them? There was absolutely no way he could have known either at that point. He proceeded to tell me that the angelic presences I had been working with were trying to help me, but that my doubts, about myself primarily, were getting in the way. He also told me that in the next few months I could expect help with my finances, in the form of a new angel--who I would "recognize when she appeared."

Well, I went back home to the states and continued on with my very difficult existence as a physician working in a super high volume, high speed, high pressure internal medicine practice serving the indigent and the Vietnamese Medicaid patients in the inner city of Denver--under a harsh and unforgiving head physician. My life at that point was dreary, depressing, and profoundly exhausting. And very poor, in that I had huge payments regularly due for past loans and obligations and was paid an almost ridiculously low wage.

It seemed as though things had gotten just about as hopeless as they could be, when I got on the plane for the last speaking venue of the year, a series of talks at the large Unity church in Austin, Texas, Unity Church of the Hills. After the lectures, I always offered personal sessions during the day in order to make a little extra. At one of the last sessions, a striking woman entered the room, sparkling with energy and high-frequency vibrations. As she seated herself,

I made note of her extraordinary sense of grace and poise, as well as her low-key, albeit brilliant, positivity, and caught myself wondering "who is this person?" She knew something.

The first thing out of her mouth was, "I have absolutely no idea why I am here." Nothing particularly unusual about that. Half the people who come to see me as a life coach say the same thing, that a friend, or a dream, or some other mystical force has stimulated them to visit me, and that they didn't know precisely why they were there yet. What was unusual about Jean is how quickly we both figured out why she was there.

I didn't know it at the time, but she was there, in part, to be my angel, and to save me from the downward spiral that had been plaguing me.

"I want to do what you do," she said, "I want to write a book and give workshops". This is not an unheard of response, although it is uncommon. What was unusual about Jean's response is the degree of commitment, the degree of conviction, I heard in her voice. This was something the woman was going to accomplish. She had obviously successfully accomplished many other things and she was going to do whatever she set her mind to.

Twenty-five minutes later, with five remaining, I decided to turn the conversation to a different direction, one which I had rarely allowed in all my experience as a life coach over the last twenty years. I found her to be so articulate and high energy and her life's story to be so compelling that I asked her if she would like to co-author a book with me. I would help her get her first book up and running if she would have her accounting firm handle my finances. With little hesitation, we both agreed to this symbiotic arrangement.

How could I make such a decision so quickly and with such certainty? That part was easy. It was all about who Jean really is. I heard her story and I knew that I had found an angelic being that had the touch of gold--as well as a heart of gold. An infinitely rare and precious combination of powers.

She was orphaned, was a high school drop out and never finished college, was married at 14, had a child with birth defects at 15 (she was a virgin when she got married....she actually wanted to get married, she did not have to!!), flew to Germany with her child to be with her husband who had joined the military when she was 16 and flew back to the States at 16 with her son to escape her then-abusive husband with the clothes on her back and a small suitcase for her son. Fast forward life 30 years. Jean has her CPA license as well as her CFP license, has started three successful businesses, sold two at a nice profit and still has her third business, a CPA firm with 20+ employees and two partners, one of whom she has worked with for over 20 years. Talk about wildly successful!!

The woman has a special touch. Everything she touches turns to gold.

But it wasn't all that easy…there was more tragedy. Over eleven years ago she experienced a violent automobile collision which very nearly killed her (details in the Preface). But even that didn't stop her. In a nearly superhuman recovery effort, she made her severe head injury work for her in a positive way. Her struggle with that long recovery process just made her that much more compassionate and more heart-centered--not to mention more grateful, for life itself.

Although brief long-distant encounters like the one I had with Jean usually turn out to wither away and turn into nothing, we both kept to the plan. Her firm handled every aspect of my finances, taxes, IRS conversations and so forth, and I helped her get her book going and, ultimately, completed. Like most people, Jean had to struggle to learn, and to lift her writing skills to a professional level. Believe me, it can be a real bear to train yourself to sit down and actually write stuff. But her mind was set and she wasn't about to let anything stop her. She kept to the lessons and worked through them to the point where she was finally turning out fascinating stories and deadly accurate advice-- about all things financial. She says I was one of her angels & she has convinced me….it was easy to pass along the knowledge that I personally paid dearly for.

Now, she is far, far more than a mere accountant, not that being a CPA isn't a major thing in and of itself. Jean Carpenter-Backus has become a highly unusual and multifaceted financial healer. Her first priority on meeting a new client is not the client's assets and liabilities or wealth. Far from it. Now, her first priority is reducing the client's anxiety – regardless of the level of wealth. For after all, fear in any form, sends out terrible messages to the universe, causing it to unfold in highly unfavorable ways. Jean knows all about the metaphysical aspects of money, understands the great laws of prosperity, and otherwise has an extraordinarily advanced calming, healing presence that far transcends the evolutionary level of any other financial professional I have ever listened to.

In fact, as soon as I started working with her, money seemed to begin flowing towards me naturally, as though during my interactions with her, a palpable amount of her "magic," her undeniable magnetism, had somehow rubbed off on me, weird as that may seem. But it was undeniably true. Money started turning up in unexpected ways at unexpected times. I would learn that this could happen in many different ways.

Sometimes it would be a bill that turned out to be in error and did not need payment. Sometimes it was Jean finding previously undisclosed deductions on my old tax returns. (Yes, there are professionals that are so thorough they actually check your old stuff). Sometimes it just turned out as a refund check or the unlikely sale of my house in a bad market. By now I realize that Jean automatically confers some of her high frequency financial energy in infinitely variable ways. I'm not sure she even understands her full capabilities as yet. But you might keep your eye on this woman.

Now she has a book. Now she has successfully started her business as a teacher and writer and--her real life's work—she has a message: showing other people how to understand, how to really "get it," about the money that flows in and through and out of their lives. And like all great teachers, she has simplified her lessons about money into a series of ten carefully sequenced recommendations. Knowing what I now know, you simply cannot afford to miss the learning of these steps and knowing how to live them. Please listen very carefully to what she has to say, and make a decent effort to put her advice into practice.

In prosperity,
Dr. Todd Michael

PREFACE

I remember the day my world shattered into a million pieces and my path was forever altered. Driving to work at 7:15am, April 9th, I plunged headlong toward miracles I could never have foreseen.

Bubbling with excitement I enjoyed the spring morning, drinking in the colors of wildflowers that draped the Austin highway like a tapestry. Pale Texas Bluebonnets and orange Indian Paintbrush bloom spectacularly in April and springtime exudes an unmistakable sweetness.

The weather was 70 degrees and foggy with a light drizzle that glistened on the highway. I smiled, thinking, "Six days until the end of tax season!" A tax accountant, I worked brutal hours this time of year and I sensed with palpable excitement through a fog of overwork that I neared the end.

An 8:15am appointment with a client who sold French furniture was to be my last meeting prior to the April 15 deadline. Excited, I told my husband as we got ready for work that after "one last meeting" I'd be able to focus on getting the work out.

I stopped at a little coffee shop. It was new

and they'd done a first class job of decorating with tables and chairs where one could sit and read the paper. The double doors swung open and the aroma of roasted beans slapped my face with smile. I made a mental note to come back when I had more time to read the paper over coffee at my leisure.

But not today. Not today.

My latte was ready. I paid, waved goodbye and got back into my car, put the latte in the cup holder, started the engine and resumed my thirty-minute journey to the office. Favorite music playing in the background, I chose the scenic route to work. Although this was a path I rarely took, I chose it because it wrapped around a beautiful subdivision and golf course. The tricky part would be crossing Southwest Parkway. Yesterday's two-lane country road was now a four-lane super-highway.

Springtime. New life.

I stopped at the stop sign, looked both ways and crossed Southwest Parkway listening to music and sipping my latte. I would arrive at the office a little ahead of my 8:15 appointment. I never saw the convertible Sebring doing seventy miles per hour. They tell me it was white.

My husband Andrew remembers hearing the radio report about a serious accident on

Southwest Parkway. He said a silent prayer for those involved but didn't give it any more thought since he didn't know anyone who traveled that route. Driving blithely to work, he was shocked when his phone jangled unexpectedly.

It was my assistant, Chris. "Andrew, have you seen Jean? Her 8:15 has been here for nearly fifteen minutes. And you know Jean's never late without calling." In a moment of clarity Andrew remembered I had left around 7:15 and that I was completely focused on my 8:15 "last" appointment. "Have you checked with the hospitals?" he asked.

Where the heck had that thought come from?

Chris laughed with gallows laughter. "No… the phones have been ringing off of the hook."

"Well, maybe she got hung up at a coffee shop or stuck in traffic. I'm sure she'll be there soon."

They got off the phone and Andrew continued driving to San Antonio. He tried calling my cell phone but kept getting only voice mail. It made no sense. The more he thought about it, the more he knew something was wrong.

"There's no way Jean would be 15 minutes late for that meeting without calling the office with an explanation." Voice mail again.

He pulled over to the side of the road, his heart beating rapidly. He called Chris, "Has Jean shown up yet?"

"No, and the clients are annoyed,"

"Have you checked with any hospitals?"

"Never crossed my mind. But I've tried her cell phone and it just goes to voice mail."

Andrew realized Chris wasn't picking up on his level of concern due to being buried in the thick of tax season. His next call was to the Austin police department. They asked him for the VIN number of my car, as if anyone carries their spouse's VIN number with them! After calling our insurance company and getting the VIN number for the wrong vehicle, one of the police operators took pity on him and said accident victims are generally taking to Brackenridge Hospital.

Andrew phoned Brackenridge and said he was trying to find his wife, Jean Backus, who hadn't shown up for work. He was put on hold until a woman came on the line and said, "I'm a social worker at the hospital, and I understand you're looking for Jean Backus. To whom am I speaking?"

In that instant, Andrew knew I was there. His final hope was that she would tell him my injuries were minor and that all this was just silly red tape.

She said I was there, that I had been in a serious accident and was in intensive care but was conscious and was asking for him. Andrew headed for the hospital. We had been married one year.

The Sebring T-boned my Camry in the passenger-side and the front seat reduced to one third its width.

My hips went left as my head and upper body whipped to the right. My head was traveling 70mph toward the passenger side of my car, certain to be cracked open like a watermelon falling off a truck.

If there's such a thing as a guardian angel, mine understood the changing geometry of collapsing steel, opposing forces, flying glass and flying objects. The passenger seat headrest altered the trajectory of my head and kept it from hitting the passenger doorpost. My head slammed instead into the shoulder belt bracket, but at a reduced speed due to the intervention of the headrest. The impact was severe enough to leave part of my scalp in the seatbelt harness and give me a brain contusion on the right side of my head. My brain bounced around inside my skull enough to cause internal bleeding and an injury to my brainstem as well.

Unconscious, my right foot hit the gas pedal and shot my car toward a vacant lot on the far side of the highway, giving me a second chance to die. There was a 35-foot cliff at the back of the lot and little to stop me from tumbling down it.

Luckily, as my car sped across rough ground my foot slipped off the accelerator and my car was stopped by a thick shrub barely five feet from cliff's edge.

The bottom of my Styrofoam latte cup remained in the console, neatly severed from the upper half, its foamy contents splashed across the windshield. My car was half its former width. A passenger would have been instantly crushed.

When the police arrived, they studied the scene and scratched their heads. "What's that Camry doing on top the hill in that vacant lot?"

The white Sebring convertible had spun 90-degrees and run into a Suburban that was stopped on the other side of the intersection. The Sebring's front end was crashed, but the Suburban was barely scratched. It appeared the Sebring and the Suburban had hit head-on.

"What's that Camry doing on top the hill in that vacant lot?"

I drive through that intersection today and feel nothing. *Nothing.* I try to remember *anything* as I drive through it now. It seems strange to me that I should feel so little in the place where I nearly died, the place where my life was forever transformed.

I was lucky. My entire central nervous system was rearranged and my neural pathways were disrupted. They told me later that my short-term memory and balance were completely wiped out. I know also that my anger, hate and negativity were surgically excised from mind and soul. Into the void where they'd been rushed feelings of pure love, wisdom, joy, and a childlike, playful essence. I couldn't conjure a negative thought! Not one.

You might be tempted to think it was the drugs. And that might explain what happened early on. But it doesn't explain the *persistence* of this profound state after every trace of medication had long faded away.

People who visited me in the hospital later told me they expected me to be daffy and watched for "brain injury" signs. You know the ones. They expected my words to slur or my mouth to drool. What they got instead was a new, improved me! All I remember is feeling angelic and loving.

Have you ever been with a good friend and

felt like you had to hurry your stories because there just didn't seem to be enough time? I've had those conversations more often than I care to remember. But true friendship takes the time, whatever time it takes, and *makes* that precious time *quality* time.

Quality time with love poured into the mix makes a big difference. Time sings as it flies because there's nothing in the world you'd rather be doing. It's the perfect moment, a defining moment. Something you never forget.

I'm not saying I changed anyone's life while I was in the hospital other than my own. But at every moment I felt present, filled with genuine interest and unconditional love. It seemed as though God came to the hospital, scooped me up, took me to heaven, taught me about love, then gently placed me back into my life in Austin, Texas, and said, "Now go *be*."

We're not supposed to remember these things and I wouldn't claim it for the longest time. "I was brain injured," I'd say to myself. "For crying out loud, stop trying to give that period of time some sort of special meaning! You were brain injured and, well, a little nutty. So stop it and move on."

That's what I said and tried to believe. For

over 13 years. Until now.

My neurologist told me that most people are either physically, emotionally or financially devastated by the injuries I had. Most suffer deeply in permanently debilitating, painful situations for the rest of their lives.

I went somewhere a little different. I went into euphoria. I'm certainly not the only person ever to go into euphoria after a brain injury. Other cases have been documented, but we're so few that the medical professionals really didn't know what to do with me.

You're wondering what this has to do with prosperity, right? I'll admit it took me a decade to put all the pieces together. But now I see clearly and want to share what I see with others.

At worst, it's a good story. At best, it will transform your financial life.

Here's the key that will unlock the truth of my story and the financial healing you're about to experience: *It all has to start... with love.*

Read on.

Jean Carpenter-Backus

Introducing the Steps to Financial Freedom

Recently, I was asked to be a presenter at a really great women's retreat titled, "Money, Sex & Chocolate." I was presenting the "Money" part, of course, although I secretly longed to delve more into the "chocolate" aspect of things. As the owner of an accounting firm with many first-rate accountants and financial advisors—and nearly two thousand fascinating clients nationally, with an amazing spectrum of equally fascinating issues--I have accumulated an enormous amount of financial information over the years. Much of this material is about investing, tax deductions, retirement planning, and other standard elements of the financial realm. But there is more, so much more.

As I scanned through shelf after shelf of this material, something struck me, something that I had long realized yet hadn't really considered in depth: Although I could find a massive amount of information available on the technical aspects of finance, taxes, etc., precious little addressed what actually drives the money equation – the emotions, the chocolate, if you will. I realized suddenly how much I had learned informally over the years about the psychological aspects of money; the feelings, the fears, the greed, the hopes, the financial maturity, and the other sentiments that so powerfully affect our perceptions of the money that flows through our lives. "What could possibly be more important," I thought to myself, "than learning how to understand and effectively manage these powerful components of our financial decisions and actions?"

Desjardins Ego/Identity Unified Model[1]

As I waded into the preparations for my talk, I recalled the terrific theory, the model, taught to me over fifteen years ago by my spiritual mentors, Liliane and Gilles Desjardins, a model referred to as the *Desjardins Model*[1]. I have applied this model over and over to a wide range of financial problems. Again and again this model has proven itself so useful that it has come to be the very foundation of my entire approach to finance. One of the greatest things about this powerful model is its elegant simplicity: Like all truly great theoretical approaches, the *Desjardins Model* makes a lot of *common sense* and is very easy to understand. This distinguishes the *Desjardins Model* from many other psychological approaches, which can easily end up being unnecessarily convoluted and hyper-cerebrated.

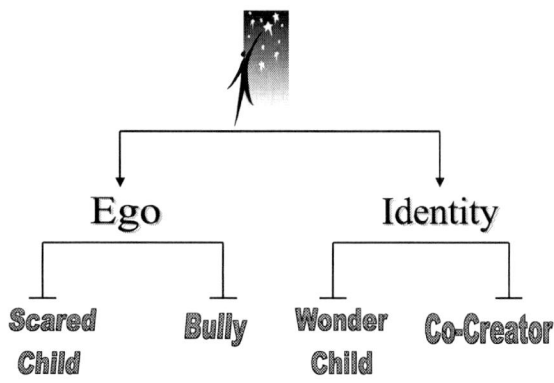

Ego & Identity

OK. Here is how the *Desjardins Model* works: Think of your self as having two parts. One part is the *ego* and the other part is the *identity*. The ego is the little "me" and the identity is the *real* "me," the real self which merges with the Infinite Intelligence that infuses the universe all around us. The ego is made up of two characters called "the scared child" and "the bully." The scared child has security issues and is always suffering in some way.

It is a "feeling" entity plagued by fear, riddled with doubt and fraught with anxiety.

People then manufacture the bully to protect their scared child. The bully is all about action and loves drama, control, sensation and medicating the scared child's feelings. Whereas the scared child is extremely fearful, the bully is aggressive—just as aggressive as the scared child is fearful. In other words, the more fearful the scared child is the bigger and meaner spirited the bully is.

The *identity* is also divided into two parts: The "wonder child" and the "co-creator." The *scared* child in the ego turns into the *wonder* child in the identity. If the energy and attention, which is being directed to the scared child, is transmuted to its positive counterpart in the identity, the wonder child emerges and the scared child fades into nothingness. The wonder child is authentic, fun, innocent, patient and relaxed. It's everything the scared child wishes it could be. Likewise, the bully in the ego turns into the co-creator in the identity. In other words, if the energy and attention that is creating and sustaining the bully is transmuted to a more positive form in the identity, the co-creator emerges. The co-creator is confident, competent, creative, disciplined and realistic. Rather than using force and control to achieve its goals, it invites, suggests and encourages.

If this seems complicated, I can assure you that it is not. The main thing that you have to do to understand the theory is to begin *applying* it. As you work the principles of the theory and apply them to real life situations, it will quickly become clear. Soon you will see how to heal the problems that are holding you back from financial freedom, which is your true destiny. Let's begin with a very simple diagram that outlines the characteristics of the ego and identity according to the *Desjardins Model* followed by an example that will illustrate each character.

Ego/Identity Characteristics[1]

Ego

Scared Child/Little Kid	***Bully/Rebel***
Fear	Power
Guilt	Control
Anxiety	Aggressive

Identity

Wonder Child/Fun	***Co-Creator***
Spontaneous	Competent
Loving	Responsible
Playful	Confident

The Scared Child

I am the owner of my business. Let's say I had a great weekend shopping. I spent quite a bit of money, but while I was relaxing and enjoying myself, I failed to keep track of my expenditures. Sure, I am enjoying my purchases now, but there is a little voice in my head saying, "You spent a lot of money and you didn't keep track of it." This little voice is not only irritating me, I begin to find that it is actually frightening me as time wears on. I experience this fear as a sort of free-floating anxiety. Instead of feeling my usual sense of security and confidence, I am apprehensive, uneasy, insecure, and have a very uncomfortable feeling of foreboding.

So, on Monday morning when I get to work, I am now all of a sudden *afraid* that I will not get paid. I have somehow *transferred* my concern about the weekend's overspending, this large amount of money going *out,* to an irrational and fearful concern about not having enough money coming *in*. As time goes by, and the longer I avoid dealing with this fear, the more the fear actually escalates.

If I continue in my avoidance behavior, leaving these escalating feelings unchecked, they may very well cause me to take some kind of action that is out of proportion to the situation. I might start anxiously reviewing my company's accounts receivable to see who owes our firm money--especially clients who are late with their payments. Imagine how odd this is, too, the owner of a company personally fretting about individual accounts! The fear that I am experiencing as the Scared Child will make me do some pretty weird and inappropriate things, just like the anxiety that you experience about your own finances and checking account might make *you* think and do some irrational and inappropriate things at times when you are in the Scared Child mode.

In my case, I might very well start becoming fearful of not receiving enough money in our firm to pay *both* my company's bills *and* me. If I let things go long enough, and my fear grows to a very intense level, I might start actually phoning clients to send payment, even though I am the CEO! These unchecked feelings of my Scared Child persona will make me extremely insecure and could bring about immense suffering.

The Bully

Because my scared child feels alone, my Bully steps up to the plate and goes into action. "No one can do it like *me*," my inner voices exclaim, so my Bully feels there is no rational alternative but to take over and straighten things out. Don't let the term "Bully" mislead you. The Bully persona has more to it than simple aggression and assertiveness. In order to get its way, the Bully can actually be very diplomatic and clever when called for. Diplomacy, after all, can be an extremely effective strategy. And because the Bully sees its main job as getting its way—in this case collecting money—it may well try an indirect and tactful approach if that appears to be the most effective route.

The Bully also loves drama and theatrics. It has a strong tendency to employ sensational and spectacular maneuvers to manipulate others in order to get its way. If these tactics succeed, and they often do, then all is well. However, if savoir-faire fails, then the bully feels as though it is left with no choice but to begin throwing its weight around. In a sense, the bully is very protective—of the scared child.

If people do not respond in the way that my Bully wishes them to, it can readily become mean-spirited, sarcastic, and pushy. The Bully absolutely hates to lose. It can be a real baby if it doesn't get its way—albeit an 800-pound baby! It will fight and fight vigorously, persistently, and effectively if it has to, no matter how low it's required to sink.

You can use your imagination to see where things go if the Bully and the Scared Child, left on automatic pilot, continue to say and do things that tend to be irrational, immature, and ineffective! In the case of the extravagant weekend and my flailing and utterly inappropriate attempts to get my clients to cough up payments, I may well make a royal fool of myself, even though I satisfy my fears in the short term. Worse yet, I may damage relationships with important clients and end up *losing* money in the long term by losing long-standing and lucrative accounts. Suffice it to say that people really don't like dealing with either the Scared Child or the Bully as they can be somewhat annoying--or downright obnoxious.

None of this really needs to happen. Instead, if I am able to "wake up" and become fully conscious of what is really going on within myself--if I can see the scared child for what it is, if I can see the bully for what it is--I can then stand back, take a deep breath to calm and center myself, and *change* the way I am reacting.

But in order for this to happen, I need to become acutely aware of my fear for what it really is. *Just as soon as I begin to feel it*, I need to *admit* to myself, right away—before things get too far out of hand--that I am reacting to my fear of overspending as a Scared Child and that my Bully is coming alive and taking action.

If I do this, if I wake up and see things for what they really are, *I can now make a conscious decision*, a very important conscious decision. I can actually *choose* to transmute my ego, my small self, which manifests as the Scared Child and the Bully, into my Identity--my true or larger self.

The Wonder Child

Let's go back to the weekend of my enjoyable shopping trip. The moment right before irrational fear whispered in my ear I only focused on the fun and good times flowing in and out of my shopping bags. My wonder child operated in high gear. Everything around me seemed like a new possibility to explore, a relaxing break from the pressure of work. That attitude came to a screeching halt when I listened to the voice of panic.

What if I had listened to my wonder child instead? It's not dominated by anxiety and worry. It would have recognized that I hadn't kept track of my expenditures and thought about taking a break to make sure I hadn't overspent. If I had overspent, the reaction of my wonder child still doesn't lead to panic. It just calmly recognizes the mistake so that I don't make it in the future and reminds me that more money will be available soon for that kind of fun. In short, it leads me to continue relaxing, even when my circumstances aren't perfect at the present moment and will lead me to more mature decisions.

The Co-Creator

It's at this point of relaxation and vulnerability where the part of my identity that is called the "Co-Creator" can awaken and take over. In my Identity, my *real* self, I actually know everything will be okay and that I will be taken care of. My Co-Creator persona is wise and calm and mature. My Co-Creator knows that I have employees that competently handle the firm's accounts receivable. My Co-Creator is realistic and knows that the suffering and negative drama my ego's personas can get into are a waste of my time and energy. It knows that this same energy can be channeled into a rational and workable solution. It simply starts making a plan to stop overspending in the short term and find a way to have fun that is affordable. The positive energy gained from those actions only encourages me to treat my clients with patience and trust that my staff will help me get our accounts resolved.

Now, you may very well say at this point that it sounds quite overly simplistic to in any way suggest that a person can somehow simply "transmute" to a higher level of consciousness right in the middle of a very fearful and upsetting drama. As everyone knows, when the drama is actually playing itself out in real life, the emotions involved can be extremely intense. The entire body may be involved in the fear response, muscles tensing, nerves trembling, solar plexus tightening in a powerful knot, and the brain…well; the poor brain at this point is a complete and total mess. How on earth does anyone expect to believe that in the middle of this powerful meltdown I can simply "wake up," have a little talk with myself and smoothly slip into my better personas, while my ultra complex and often times deep-seated neuroses are raging all through my body and mind? Isn't this a rather Pollyanna and unrealistic approach? If it were that simple why doesn't everyone know about this?

The answer isn't in the theory, even though the process is relatively simple, in the sense that it can be readily understood at an *intellectual* level. The actual art and skill of *doing* what is necessary takes a bit of time and practice to master. But it *can* be mastered. Any sincere person who has endured enough financially painful bouts of insanity or is sufficiently motivated to learn, practice and persist can operate in their true identity. There are obviously many systems for dealing with fearful and irrational states of mind that cause a person to act in ways that are destructive, particularly with regard to their personal finances. But the *Desjardins Model*, this new way of thinking about your self and its reactions to the world's stressors, just plain *works*. It does. You'll have to try it, work at it, *and apply* it to real-life situations, but as you do you'll see that it's true. Did you really think it would be as easy as snapping your fingers?

You read about my own little scenario, with the weekend's overspending and the resultant anxiety and irrational, desperate behaviors that manifested. Your own scenarios will differ, of course, but as soon as you start to take a hard look at your own life and your own dramas, you will easily be able to identify the Scared Child, the Bully and even the Identities personas: The Wonder Child and the Co Creator. A very simple example might be you sitting down in the part of the month when you have to sort out your bills and balance your checking account.

If you are under financial duress, and you almost certainly are to some degree, or you wouldn't be reading this book in the first place, you might find that your bills seem overwhelming, your account won't balance and/or you don't have nearly enough money to make ends meet. What happens? Typically you will become very anxious, right? Well, the anxious "you" that is reacting in this way is the Scared Child.

As you continue to watch yourself over the next few hours or days, you may likely then observe the Bully persona emerging and making itself known. You may start yelling at the spouse or the kids to stop spending in some way, or you might start a quarrel with someone at the phone company about your "excessive bill." It's really not all that difficult to begin to see how this works in your own life, and there will be explicit exercises later in the book where you can really start to understand how the Desjardins Model works and how you can apply it to your own real life situations.

The really important part of these exercises will be to learn how to "switch on" your Identity, by deliberately going into your Wonder Child and Co-Creator personas. The Wonder Child and Co-Creator are extremely successful beings. These are the parts of you that can become a money magnet, get the better job, sell the house, land the big account, and win the contest! As we said, although transmuting your very anxious and sometimes aggressive Scared Child and Bully personas into these more beneficial personas is a bit difficult, it is hardly impossible and something that any reasonable person can learn with a little practice. And that most certainly includes *you!*

True Story #1
"You Don't Have To Worry About Money In This Lifetime"

When I first met with him, Steve was an attorney. His wife, Zelda, was a realtor. They had two kids and were in the upper end of middle-America. Although they pulled in good incomes together, they were frustrated because their money would just evaporate at the end of each month. I had a strong suspicion, and told them, that they did not need to worry about money in this lifetime. I had no idea where this thought came from and before I could stop myself those words came out of my mouth. I felt a bit silly as I tried to find any shred of evidence in their financial life to support this. Although I saw no evidence, I had a knowing that was so familiar, an intuition that I had come to trust. Nothing weird. They wanted to agree with me; however, they saw what I saw and just shook their heads.

I could sense the brazen stress between them. She was mad at Steve because she thought he could easily make more money so that she could cut back on her hours at work and spend more time with the kids. After all, he *was* self employed and set his own hours. While her cell phone rang evenings and weekends due to the nature of her work, he would walk in the door at home each day at precisely 5:30pm, finished with work and ready for his supper. He knew he made a good income and felt like he was doing the best he could. Although he supported the idea of her working less, he felt maxed out and was unwilling to work the brutal hours necessary to make up for her decreased income. Quality of life was more important to him.

They could not resolve the money issue and grew further apart until they were quite bitter and had nothing nice to say to each other. Their relationship completely deteriorated when Steve started talking about closing his practice and going into commercial real estate development. His instincts told him that this could be wildly lucrative if he could just hold on until the Austin real estate market rejuvenated. He did shut down his practice and started investing every penny he could find into the commercial real estate market. He was even borrowing money from his parents. Zelda watched him in fear and disgust. She gritted her teeth in despair as their debt mounted.

They were in my office when he asked her to give him part of her $40,000 certificate of deposit when it matured to put into another real estate deal. She broke down in tears again. She would never, ever give him any of that money to watch him throw it away in real estate. It would be less painful to just flush it down the toilet, she thought. Daily meltdowns became her way of coping as she witnessed their relationship wreckage and their finances in ruins. She could not support him, did not want to support him and was livid with what she saw as his addiction to the next real estate deal. She lost complete faith in him and could barely even look at him anymore without feeling incredible rage and utter helplessness.

As they sat in my office, I felt compelled to tell them again that they did not have to worry about money in this lifetime. I still had no idea where this obviously ridiculous thought came from as I saw even less evidence in their life to support it, yet I believed it with all my heart.

After their divorce, he would call me periodically when he would feel financially insecure and ask me to "say that again." I would tell him that he did not have to worry about money. By now, he was in about eight to ten real estate development projects, most of which he would put together with his partner, Abel, a good friend since law school. Occasionally, when Steve had no money to invest, he would get an interest in the real estate in exchange for finding the deal and putting it together.

Let's fast forward life about ten years into the future. This is the truth. Both of his kids are now finished with college and are doing well on their own. The Austin real estate market eventually took a turn for the best. Steve cashed in nearly all of his real estate projects (at the peak of the market). He is now a multi-millionaire and lives in a different state with his fiancée. They just closed on a beautiful $1.5 million dollar home. Life is good.

Zelda stayed with our firm for six or seven years after the divorce. She was awarded half of the real estate deals pursuant to the divorce decree. She thought they were a joke and was anxiously waiting until she could write them off as a loss on her taxes. When Steve sold the projects and Zelda ended up a multi millionaire as well, she put Steve in a new light. She had a newfound respect for him and felt ashamed & embarrassed that she had not supported him during the marriage.

I am still his accountant and he still calls me to hear, "You don't need to worry about money in this lifetime." We laugh about it now. I think it is important to have people in your life that can see for you what you can't see for yourself. If you ever have a strong, positive intuition about someone, TELL THEM!

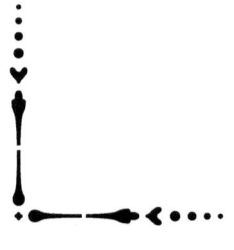

True Story #2
"Your Finances Will Mirror What You Think About"

When I first met with Ann, she was frustrated because she couldn't figure out how to pull more money from her successful salon/day spa business. Every time the salon's sales increased, the overhead seemed to increase even more leaving less money for her to take. Fortunately, her lease would expire within a year and she was already starting to look for a more appropriate space, itching to be out of there. She had signed a seven year lease on her current space against her better instincts screaming "don't do it…stop *now* - you'll regret it!" She realized that she signed the lease out of fear. She rationalized it was better to secure a lease that was 75% adequate rather than risk looking for another space and losing this space while not finding a space that was better. After seven years she promised herself that she would listen to that little voice next time and not repeat this mistake that she regretted for way too long. The parking was inadequate and the landlord was impossible – repairs took forever. One time during a hard rain, her ceiling started leaking. Three days later, the pail to catch the water was replaced by a barrel while the ceiling was stained and ruined. This was a horrible reflection on her business. Yes, she needed to get out of here. Maybe now she will learn to pay attention and listen to that little voice called intuition. She was determined to get past this fear that seemed to run her financial life, was exhausting and left her feeling insecure and in fight-or-flight mode. Thank God she could at least label it now. She was sick of it.

She and I would get together to discuss taxes, her finances & goals, etc. I would review the business financial statements and her personal cash flow. We would brainstorm, review goals and see how much in alignment her decisions were with her goals. As her fear mounted, I would see her jaw tighten. She would try to rationalize and justify her fear. It was amazing how strong and clever this sabotaging part of her was. It kept me on my toes. I had to pay attention otherwise I would go down the same path of fear she was on and we would start agreeing and planning together based on fear rather than reality. It was important that I point out reality because it did not resemble the picture her fear had in the least. She would try the "Yeah, but" scenarios; however, there was more evidence pointing toward financial health than otherwise. She eventually woke up and learned how to see her finances through the lens of reality rather than her fear. Not that her fear doesn't haunt her now and then. It does and it is pretty tricky; however, it does not dominate like it used to.

She took her time looking for the new space and did not settle for the space that was 75% acceptable. She has been in her new space for nearly two years. It is double the size of her previous space and has a parking garage. It is in a popular district of Austin and her business has nearly doubled in size. Interesting, when she started seeing reality, her business became much more profitable. She realized that the profitability of her business is a direct reflection of her internal pictures. When she was in her fear, she made quick decisions just to give herself some relief even though the decisions were not in her best interest and led to sabotage. Now that she is more confident and less fearful, her decisions are based on reviewing all the facts, taking her time and choosing the option that best suits her situation.

She is genuinely happy, has gratitude and now takes the time to have a quality life including golf once a week with me!

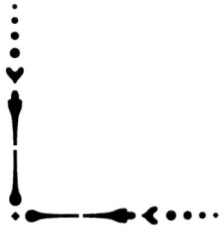

PROSPERITY CYCLE

Ten Steps to Financial Freedom

Step One
Wake Up!

Have you ever heard the saying, "If you want your dreams to come true, you have to wake up?" Sit back, close your eyes and in your mind's eye scan your finances. That's it. - the checking account, the debit card, the cash withdrawals, the income, the mortgage, the credit card balances, etc., If you are experiencing anything less than complete abundance, you are *not* truly awake. An additional issue complicates this problem: you don't even know you're not awake!

As you work through this chapter you will come to see how this is, indeed, quite true. The fact is that your current state of "financial sleep" is why the abundant, flowing, pleasurable, fun-packed, love-filled personal reality you *want* to be living—is failing to manifest as reality. It's why your cherished dreams continue to evade you, like a horizon, blue into blue into blue, perpetually receding beyond your reach. What you think you "know" isn't working. Is it? As Yogi Berra said, "The problem ain't what you don't know;

it's what you know that ain't so."

Volumes can be said about how dreams can be made to happen. But for now, forget everything that you know, or think that you "know." This will put you in a beginner's state of mind, transforming you into a person who can actually learn. It is terribly important that you get into this *beginner's mind*; to become as a child, eager to learn a completely new and different way of thinking and acting with regards to your personal finances.

Right now, with the naïve curiosity and trust of a child, you are going to fully awaken your ability to imagine--to *image-in*. Performing the following exercise will begin to make you more aware of this amazing faculty. Human beings are the only species that we know that have the ability to see how things can be. This includes the ability to see how things might be in the future, to purposely form and manipulate mental images of things that are not yet physically "real" in the here and now. Doing the following exercise will help you start to harness and put to use your ability to form images by helping you awaken to your potential.

Awakening!

Start the exercise by settling yourself somewhere you are comfortable and free of any significant distractions. Now, close your eyes and begin to use that amazing and powerful part of your mind that forms images—your imagination.

See your checking account. See what that account really is. See what is in it. See how it flows and moves and responds to your life, your energy and your intentions.

What do you see? Do you "see" the energy in your account as visual images or do you "see" the energy with your body as a kind of feeling?

Do you see energy? If so, is it moving, flowing? What does the energy look like? Look and look harder.

Do you see a mess? Do you see order to the energy or disorder? Does the energy in your account connect to the rest of the world? Where does the energy in your checking account come from? Where does it originate? What does it do while it is in your account? Then, where does the energy go?

If you cannot answer these questions fully and completely, if you cannot *see* everything with perfect clarity and precision, great! You're starting to become aware of the *mystery* of it all. You are starting to see how much you don't know, how much you have to learn with your beginner's mind. As the movie *What the Bleep Do We Know* pointed out, the more we study reality, the more we run up against a "wall of mystery," the world of mysteries and mysteries *within* mysteries. Let's continue the exercise and go further into the mystery.

Look again into your checking account. Then look harder. You are waking up. You are lifting yourself out of denial, becoming increasingly more and more conscious of the "reality" of your checking account. Can you see the energy in your account as a kind of life force? Can you see that it is alive?

Now, see the "money energy" in your account connecting to the outside world, the world you live in, the personal reality that is your everyday life. Where does this "money energy" of your account come from?

See the sources as though you were in a pond fed by mountain streams. Imagine that you are examining the landscape upstream, looking for every source of the streams that empty into your pond. See the financial system of your employer that feeds energy into your system. See any other sources and see them connecting to your financial realm, which centers around your checking account.

Wake up.
See the energy in your account
as a dynamic, living,
pulsating life force.

Continuing and deepening your awakening, see yourself awakening in the morning. What is around you? What is in your room? What are you lying on? See where all of these things came from. See the money that was used to purchase your bed. Where did it come from? What did the process of purchasing your bed look like? Where did the kitchen table come from? Was money used to purchase it? Where does the electricity come from? See the money flowing from you to the utility company to exchange for the electricity. See the money that was used to purchase your car and the gasoline that feeds it.

Continue the meditation as you move through your financial realm. See your workplace. How does the flow of money look like and feel like as it moves in and through and around your place of work? Make it real. Use your imagination.

Continue through your day seeing the flow of financial energy as it moves into and through every element of your daily life. Everywhere you look, you see the distilled and powerful potential of money flowing through your city and your home and your life like electricity through the complex circuitry of a computer. See how the money energy in your world flows like water through the infinitely intricate and convoluted elements of a mountain landscape, through the components and layers of a massive ecosystem.

Now, look even deeper. See that the energy

that is coming from your sources of money energy, such as your employer, must also have sources. See that the streams of energy flowing into your account and life from the financial system of your employer are also fed by streams of energy yet farther upstream. See that these streams go on and on, that they connect everything in your world with an incredibly potent, distilled life force.

Can you see the vast stores of energy that lie upstream? Can you see how they all interconnect? Can you see exactly where these sources are and exactly how they connect to you? Can you see exactly and precisely how you can begin to connect your own checking account your own pool of energy with these vast, nearly infinite sources of money?

"No," you say? No?

Excellent! Now you are beginning to awaken to the mystery. Now you are beginning to be conscious of the vast, incomprehensible, beautiful, and bountiful streams of money, of distilled and incredibly potent potential that are all around you, moving everywhere through your world, connecting together the people and the things within your world in an infinitely complex web of energy.

Now watch you're self. See yourself. See how you feel about this vast web of pulsating potential. Do not worry. Do not judge. There is no "right" way to see this vast network of potential. All that matters at this point is that you begin to awaken to the mystery and magnificent complexity of the money energy that flows everywhere through your world. See how much you cannot see. See how much you have to learn with your beginner's mind.

Go back to your vision of your checking account. Now see where the energy in your account goes. What does the energy of your account feed and nourish? What depends upon its reliable and steady flow? See the mortgage company that lives by the energy that you and others give it with your mortgage payments. See the financial systems of the people who perform various services for you. See how your payments to them from your checking account connect you to them, allowing them to live and grow.

See the energy in your account connecting to your world in an important way. See that these connections are real. See your account as a small part within the great network. What does this look like? What does it feel like?

Now, you are ready to awaken yet further. Now you are ready to awaken to the full power of your potential as a being that can form images. Up to this point in your meditation you have taken a passive viewpoint, seeing what is before you as things that are happening to you. But now you are going to get a taste of a different way of seeing, a different way of being conscious and awake.

Go back to the beginning of the meditation. Once again, see the living flowing energy within your checking account. How does it look...? How does it feel...?

But this time everything is different.

This time, instead of passively watching and feeling the energy of your personal portion of the great web of financial energy, make it look like you want it to look --with your imagination.

Wake up!

Your image-ination, the part of your mind that can form images, is a gift, a power that God has bestowed upon you, a power entrusted to every human being.

Wake up!

Starting with your checking account and the elements of your day-to-day life, see and feel the energy just as you would want it to be in an ideal world for you.

Imagine it having just the kind of overflowing abundance and joyful prosperity that you <u>want</u> it to have

Now you're ready to begin the process of learning what we have to offer. You've had a small taste of how big it all is, how complex and wondrous the system of money energy that flows around and through your life really is. You've had a brief experience showing you how much you don't know. And, hopefully you've grasped how powerful your own mind can be within this financial milieu.

The beginner's mind will allow you to have the same kind of new and creative and enthusiastic energy you would use if you were rebuilding and remodeling an old house. It's ready to throw everything out and start again new and fresh, building a life and a belief system that really works, a life that feels right. As you go through the steps to financial freedom, do yourself a big favor: Forget what you *think* you know. Wake up!

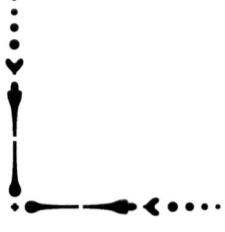

Step One - Wake Up!
Questions and Exercises

1. What does "financially waking up" mean to you?

2. Are you able to sense a bigger picture with more happening and more moving parts than you previously realized?

3. Are you ready to transform your financial life and claim the prosperity that is yours?

Step Two
Starting Point

Let's use the metaphor of planning a cross-country trip to illustrate your financial starting point. Before even taking this trip, what do you need? The first item is most likely a road map. The second item is something you do not necessarily need, but it could certainly facilitate a smoother journey. I am referring to a navigator.

Before you can do anything you need to locate where you are on the map – your starting point.

Let's apply this metaphor to your finances and perform a very simple exercise so you can get some perspective about your financial starting point. Simply get out a piece of paper and pencil or get on your computer. List and total what income you bring home each month. Then under that, list your monthly expenses and total them. When you total your estimated monthly expenses, is the amount less than your total monthly income, about break even or more? It is the cash coming into your household and cash going out of your household each month. Let's call this the "cash in/cash out" approach.

Now what is your debt picture? What do you owe, how much, and to whom? Did you include the monthly payments on the debt with the monthly expenses? If not, in order to get to an accurate starting point, they need to be included. This simple little exercise will give you information about your starting point. Again, try not to judge or evaluate. Just observe.

It is important to remove the mystery and get to the truth about where you are starting. It's just as important as locating your starting point on a map when you plan a trip. If you live in Austin, Texas and you want to go to Boulder, Colorado, you aren't going to start in New Orleans, Louisiana. You can indeed locate and trace the directions from New Orleans to Boulder but how does that help you if you live in Austin, Texas? You get the picture.

Once you've determined where you are, you need someone with you to help you get there. The best navigator is someone that understands you and communicates well. If you were taking a long trip, you would most likely select a navigator that is pleasant and even likes to have fun. Certainly you'd want someone who can read a road map! Choosing a financial advisor is no different.

My recommendation is to interview at least three financial advisors (these initial meetings should be no charge). I also suggest that you select these advisors based on a referral from people you already know, respect and admire. If you're driving and your navigator gives you directions that are over your head or that you cannot understand, where will you end up? You want someone who can interpret, translate and communicate the directions in a manner that is very easy for you to understand. You want your attention to be on the driving aspect and you want the navigator to make sure you do not take a wrong turn. It's not their responsibility to drive, but to keep you on the right road.

I suspect you would also prefer neither someone that gets so wrapped up in the details that they lose sight of the big picture nor someone that has to communicate each and every excruciating detail to you. The best financial advisor navigates you all the way to your chosen destination and doesn't abandon you because you took a wrong turn! It has to be a win/

win proposition. They win when you win. They have to care about you achieving your financial goals. Otherwise, how can you make agreements and be accountable to them?

My personal preference is someone who is a good listener and can mirror information back to me in a style that I can understand. They make things make sense with simple language, and it's easy for them to simplify complicated information. They automatically know that I don't want to spend my time and energy attempting to translate what they are telling me. They will translate and simplify the information based on a learning style that works for me. If they can't, they're not going to get me where I need to go.

Typically a financial adviser will pay for themselves many times over based not only on the expensive wrong turns they can prevent you from taking, but also in real dollars based on their recommendations and ability to brainstorm effectively. If you have that, and you know the truth of your present situation, you're ready to get going.

Step Two - Starting Point Questions and Exercises

1. If you continue on your current course, where are you headed?

2. What is your starting point? List at least five important financial things currently in your life that create your starting point.

3. Do you have a financial advisor? If not, list three people who you respect that you can ask for a recommendation.

4. Are you ready to contact them and set up an initial meeting?

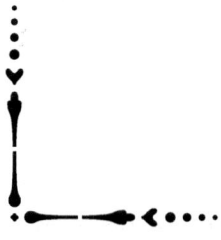

Step Three
Know the Destination

You are on a journey, an extremely important journey. And, as with any journey, it is essential to identify the destination, to *know* where you are going. That much should be clear. At least it *sounds* clear. And it *sounds* simple. However, the fact of the matter is that, although it seems incredibly obvious to always know where we are going, much of the time we really *don't*. This is particularly true of our excursions through the financial realm.

When specifically questioned on this matter, it is absolutely amazing how many individuals don't have a clearly defined financial endpoint or goal. All too often, they respond to such queries with very vague answers such as "I want to be financially secure," "I want to be rich," or "I want to be financially independent." That kind of vague thinking just isn't good enough. It's not even close. "I want to be rich" is not a destination. To continue the analogy of a person going on a road trip, "I want to be rich" or "I want to be financially secure" are analogous to a person saying,

"I want to go east," or "I want to go far." "East" is not a destination. "Far" is not an endpoint. Neither is "rich," or "secure," or "financially independent." You need to have clearly defined goals that you can measure and tell whether or not you've achieved them.

On a road trip, navigated and executed by a mature, clear thinking, sane adult, a real and useful destination would be something like, 117 Palm Grove Court, Paia, Maui, Hawaii. Similarly, a real and useful financial destination would be something like, creating an emergency fund with three to six months of living expenses, owning my house and having my mortgage paid.

Purpose. Intention. Goals. Target. Objective. Endpoint. These words make up the foundation for the entire motivational and self-help realm. In fact, the single most important piece of knowledge that a human being can ever have is that human intention actually alters reality, and that having a clearly defined goal or goals, is absolutely imperative, absolutely indispensable for success, in any realm, financial or otherwise. The decisions you make about where you want to go in life result in far more powerful effects than you can possibly imagine. The vast majority of experimental and theoretical physicists even believe now that when a human being makes a *decision*—such as deciding on a financial goal—the entire universe splits and a new universe, a kind of "child universe," if you will, is born. This may sound either crazy or ridiculous, but scientists can't seem to find any viable and reliable evidence that this is not the case.

When you make a decision—like the one you're about to make as you complete this step in your financial healing—a new world will actually form. And what is really fascinating—and really practical—is that the new world, the new personal reality you are about to create with your consciously planned intentions, may have different laws and rules. What is impossible in the personal reality you find yourself living right now may actually be possible in the new reality. Although this is perhaps the greatest core secret of all the ages, it is no longer theory espoused only by mystics and sages. It's scientific fact, hard, cold reality, as agreed upon by the most intelligent and well-educated scientific minds of the new millennium.

Every day, every minute, every second of your life, this law is shaping the fabric of your personal reality with unerring and absolute precision. You're always in one way or another "deciding" things. You decide whether to put one foot in front of another as you walk down the street. You decide whether to buy a certain item or not. You decide to turn the page of this book or not.

You cannot *not* decide things. Even when you don't decide or aren't paying much attention, even when you are being vague and uncertain, these mindsets are also varieties of "decisions." All of your thoughts have an impact on reality. And all of your reality, every single thing that you see and hear and experience in the world that has formed around you, is a perfect and absolutely precise reflection of the sum total of your decisions and the intentions that have preceded you.

The only sane thing for you to do is to set your intention, set your destination, with purpose and surety, with conviction and clarity of the highest order. The world around you always monitors and responds to what you think, what you intend and where you want to go.

The problem is that it is getting mixed signals. Wow. Mixed signals??!! That would be putting it mildly. Most of the day it gets signals that basically say, I'm not paying attention, I'm not interested, I'm powerfully influenced by my boss, my government, my partner, my job, my paycheck, the economy, the traffic on the freeway, the weather, the times… In other words, "I am a victim of circumstances."

Then, every so often, if you're lucky, a tiny portion of positive thinking comes through. The universe hears a small, tentative voice whimpering, "I want to be rich," "I want to have a big lucky break," "I intend to find the perfect job where I'll make more money," or, "I'll have the courage to approach my boss and insist on the raise I know perfectly well I have deserved for months." Sometimes we get more specific and say, "I'll put all my accounts on my computer on Quicken and make budgets and plans and keep track of every penny that flows through my life," "I'll work things so that I end up in a beautiful house which will accrue markedly in value and make me a fortune," or, "I'll cut back on a few expenditures here and there and save an extra couple hundred dollars per month," and so on and so forth.

But as the mind wanders and the pressures of the day continue, you're back to the same old barely conscious thoughts that go, "Let's get real, my boss controls everything and there is no way he is giving me or anyone a raise," "don't be ridiculous, I'll just put off saving that money another month and splurge a little this month," "who's kidding herself, my ability to manage my accounts and learn how to computerize things is very limited," or, "I have minimal talent and will never realistically learn much about investing," blah, blah, blah…

Our minds unleash a torrent of vague or outright negative self-proclamations peppered with a few half-hearted positive affirmations. Like a few drops of white paint in a gallon of jet black, the brightest it turns is a little bit gray. And you wonder why the reality that you see around you is as it is. The reason is you. It's all you. It's ALL you. Not some of it. Like Einstein said, the world is either all a miracle or it is random. Either your intentions create all of your reality, or your reality is random.

With this in mind ask yourself: Where am I going? Where have I been telling myself that I am going all day long, day after day after day?

Would you like to know the answer to that question? Look around you. Look in your checking account. Look in your savings account. Look at your paycheck. Look at your balance with the IRS. Look at you investment portfolio, or look at the fact that you don't even have one. That's where you have been telling yourself that you are going. Wherever you are right now is the exact, the EXACT sum total of all of the things that you have been telling yourself you are going. Do you like it? Or do you need to make some changes?

You can start right now, today, by changing your destination, pinning it down, honing it, meditating on it, dwelling on it, obsessing over it if necessary—to the point where your thoughts no longer contain a few drops of thin, white paint in a bucket of black, but a steadily increasing flow of concentrated, powerful, purified, and ever increasingly clear intentions. You will no longer be a victim, waiting passively for someone or something else to decide where you are going, where your endpoint will be. From now on you will tell the universe and everything around you where you will go.

Your destination is a specific, financial goal that you would like to achieve. Once you have decided on the financial goal, this is your ultimate target. You will probably have several, but take each one at a time to avoid confusion. Keep it simple. Your financial adviser can help you prioritize the goals as well as support you in achieving them. As a course is charted from your present financial situation, to your chosen destination, smaller goals or signposts along the way will let you know whether you're on or off course. Don't expect perfection. If you're off course here and there, it's completely normal as long as you are moving in the direction of your target.

Just to cement this concept and put it in context, I'll give you an example. Your goal (destination) is to pay off a credit card, a MasterCard, with a current balance of $5000. This debt causes stress and is a point of contention with your family. With that in mind, you tell your financial advisor that you want to pay this off without incurring more credit card debt in the process. The financial advisor then reviews your current financial situation (starting point) and offers various options and approaches to accomplish the goal (destination). They can also identify and communicate smaller goals along the way that will be your signposts if you're on or off track. As you work together, they may even point out the best option in their opinion, based on their history with you. This can and should be part of building a relationship with a financial adviser.

Step Three - Know the Destination Questions And Exercises

1. List three things you have been telling yourself & the world that have sabotaged your financial life.

2. Identify one, only one, financial goal. Clarify & crystallize this in your mind. Write it down.

3. Now, with your ultimate financial goal in mind, list the smaller goals that will move you in the direction of the larger goal.

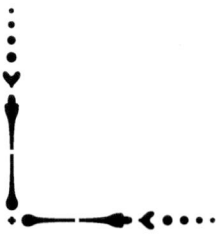

Step Four
Creating the Time Line

Of all the words that human beings use, not counting minor articles of speech such as "the" or "and," one of the most frequently used words of all is "time". We *think* about this thing that we call time more than anything else. Time, for a human being, is a measure of life. A piece of time is, in a very real sense, *a piece of your life*, a segment of your life span here on this most spectacular of worlds. And for a human being on a journey such as the one you have embarked upon, you can *use* the parameter of time, a tool of infinite versatility and power.

In Step Three we talked about the importance of clarifying and solidifying your goals, the endpoints large and small that you are deciding upon. In Step Four, you will *decide*—with equal clarity and intention—the *timing* of the events that you will manifest within your life.

But, you may well say, "How on earth can I decide when everything in my life will occur? Given the obvious elements of uncertainty that characterize life, and reality in general, how can I decide with any degree of reliability when everything is going to happen?"

You just do it. Break apart the passive victim consciousness that has caused so many problems in your life, and begin now to view time differently. Instead of waiting for things to happen, you *decide* when they will occur. It's true that many of the time frames you decide upon will not turn out to happen exactly as you have planned. So what?! A person who has set his or her will to be healed will never dwell upon this for even a second.

Don't waste your time. Your time, the amount of life that you have, is incredibly precious. Use it only to make decisions, to decide, like a miracle worker decides, when the miraculous will transpire. The more you take charge and decide the more likely things will happen when you intend them to happen. This is how your healing, your financial healing, will happen: you *choose*, you *resolve,* you *decide—what* will happen and *when* it will happen. Your goals may fail to manifest exactly when you have decided they would best happen. But rest assured that the timing will be *much* closer to the way you would like things to happen than if you gave in to the passive victim-consciousness that brought you to your present place of lack and unhappiness.

Decide when you will make your goals happen. Then, live exactly *as though* the timing is perfectly on schedule. *Act as if* everything is moving ahead with perfect precision. If something untoward happens and you suffer a setback large or small, don't lie there feeling sorry for yourself or doubting your ability to proceed. Immediately stand up, dust yourself off, adjust and keep going. Make new decisions, with new and even more powerful resolution and conviction.

> Your miracle *will* unfold with perfection to the degree that you consistently *act as if* it is unfolding with perfection.

Begin now. Of all the times that you can ever experience, *now* is the most powerful of all. Now is arguably the only real time anyway. List the goals that you came up with in Step Three. Assign times to each of these goals. Don't worry about being "realistic" or "correct." Instead, focus on what would be the best for you and your loved ones.

This is a financial road trip, similar to a real journey from Austin, Texas to Boulder, Colorado. Start with the small goals and work to the bigger goals. Your daily travel itinerary along your journey is equivalent to your short-term financial goals. For example, today you may wish to drive from Austin to Oklahoma City. That would be your short-term goal. In financial terms your first long-term goal may be to eliminate credit card debt. What short-term goals would need to be established to achieve that long-term goal? What can you do today or this month toward that goal? Many "todays" strung together can easily equal several months or years moving toward your long-term goal or not. If you have small wins along the way you are much more likely to motivate and fuel what it takes to achieve your long-term goals.

If we planned our road trip from Austin to Boulder, we would decide how long it would take to get there based on a number of factors: number of miles in total and traveled each day, where to stop and rest, type of trip desired, etc... The same basic theory applies when you plan the timeline to meet your financial goals. You determine a time line based on realistic factors. It's almost as if you back into a time line based on what is realistic.

For instance, let's say the credit card debt you want to pay off is $10,000, and your initial goal is to pay it off in two years. In order to determine if this is realistic, you would determine the amount of extra money needed to pay each month in addition to the minimum required payment in order to completely pay it off in two years. Then compare this amount to the extra amount you are realistically able come up with each month, and adjust your time line accordingly.

When you have finished, make an appointment to sit down with your financial advisor. She or he will help ensure you set realistic goals as well as identify the governing constraints. She or he may tell you that you are rushing some things while delaying others needlessly. You may have to allow for unanticipated events or other contingencies that affect your time line. If you have a family with 3 children, 2 cars and a dog, it's silly not to set aside money for car repairs, medical bills or veterinary visits. Your advisor has helped many other people and will immediately identify these kinds of adjustments to improve your plan.

Naturally, all of this is written down to keep you accountable to your goals. When you have completed Step Four carefully, and it has been completely reviewed and approved by your advisor as sound, reasonable, and workable, make a large version that can be prominently displayed above your desk or somewhere else where it is clearly and frequently seen.

Buy a 24" x 36" piece of poster board. Cut it in half lengthwise so that you have two strips, each twelve by thirty-six inches. Tape them together securely into one strip seventy-two inches long. Across the bottom with a heavy black marker and a yardstick draw a line seventy-two inches long. At the far left, put the present date. Then put a series of hash marks along the line. The lengths between hash marks may vary depending upon the total number of years you need to represent on the final timeline. A good average is about two inches per month. This will make a single year two feet long. Using a pencil so that you can erase things and adjust their positions on the timeline, enter your goals onto the timeline. When you are certain your entries accurately reflect the decisions you have made with your advisor's help, use heavy markers to neatly and boldly print your goals.

The time line you have just created is an extremely powerful tool. It can help you solidify, in your mind, the plan for your journey, from lack and all of its attendant problems to a state of vigorous prosperity. If you want to dwell on something, dwell on your timeline. Now you know where you are going *and* you have made a series of powerful and intelligent decisions that will coordinate the *timing* of all the integrated parts of your journey. But no matter how elegant your time line looks or how detailed its components, remember:

The only *real* time is NOW.

The only time that you can *act* is NOW.

The only time to move toward the state of prosperity you seek is NOW.

Today is the day and this hour is the hour. Don't procrastinate one minute longer! Look at the time line before you. Take the reins of your life and get going.

You can do it!

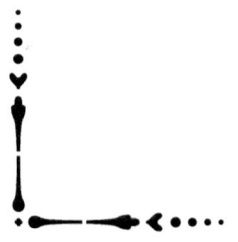

Step Four - Creating the Time Line Questions and Exercises

1. Touch money! That's right. In this day and age...with debit cards and credit cards...fewer people actually touch the green stuff anymore! Put a $50 or $100 bill in your wallet. Let it make you smile when you see it and touch it. Now that's prosperity in action!

2. Go to your bank and get some $2 bills – yes, they are still in circulation AND they make people very happy. Go get some and start giving them away as tips. Brace yourself for their reaction!

3. Follow the poster board exercise in this Chapter to help solidify your goals and time line.

Step Five
The Plan (KISSS)

I recently met with a new client who had previously worked with a local financial planner. Although they met on several occasions, this client felt as though they had made no financial progress at all. During the course of our meeting, the reason became crystal clear as to why they did not progress.

The planner they worked with filled out a standard financial planning form based on questions they asked the client. After inputting this information into the computer, they then generated a technical, complicated, generic 100-page financial plan. The planner began explaining each part of the plan that included retirement planning, kids' college planning, estate planning, investment planning, etc. As a result, the clients were quickly overwhelmed but said nothing because they "thought" they were supposed to understand and did not want to appear ignorant. After all, it was their money.

The planner started discussing various investments they were selling that would be perfect for this client based on the plan. This would be the first step toward meeting the plan's goals, which were fuzzy to them to begin with. Thankfully, my clients tuned-in to their screaming intuition to GET OUT OF THERE! Out of the several cardinal rules the financial planner had broken, the first was Keep It Simple, Simple, Simple.

In order not to overwhelm clients, a financial planner is not only responsible to keep it simple; she or he must keep it logical and understandable. It's just as important for the client to be very pro-active and involved in the plan. After all, it is YOUR plan. The best role a financial planner can play is listening and patiently guiding you though their financial maze. Actually, this is where the fun really begins and where simplicity will serve you. If you don't understand the plan, you won't achieve your goals. So let's get started on a real plan.

Remember the road trip? We now have the starting point, the destination, the estimated time line and, most importantly, we are awake. Now we will fill in the details. It makes a difference if you have a deadline. For instance, if you go to a wedding out of state, you would plan this trip differently than a vacation without the pressure of an impending deadline.

Let's go back to the example of paying off a $10,000 credit card debt. When you create a plan to pay off this credit card, you have to take certain things into consideration, like the amount of extra money you have or can create each month without jeopardizing other obligations. The plan should easily fit into the time line with a little wiggle room; therefore, the time line is flexible until the plan is created.

Say you would like to pay off this credit card debt in one year. However, the extra money you have each month to apply to this debt dictates that it will be paid off in three years rather than one. Unless another plan is created to come up with the extra money needed each month, three years will realistically be your time line. As time goes by and circumstances change, the plan can change accordingly. It should always be fluid and flexible without losing its backbone. It's organic and you breathe life into it. Over time, you can actually create a healthy relationship with the plan as it is nurtured and you experience some success. Confidence will grow with a sense of accomplishment. Imagine a life where you create, earn and are directly responsible for your financial freedom!

I want to reiterate the importance of focusing on one goal at a time and keeping it simple. When a financial plan gets too complicated, it has too many moving parts and can become cumbersome and heavy. Most of the time people abandon these types of plans because they create a sense of failure. When a plan stays light and simple, it is always easy to understand, easy to start where you left off and will feed your sense of accomplishment. It can even be fun and charismatic.

These words don't typically describe a financial plan. You will have some amount of pain (think sacrifice) in your plan. But my own experience has been that people move toward pleasure and fun and away from pain. So add some fun and make it pleasant. This type of plan is much more likely to succeed.

Step Five - The Plan (KISSS) Questions and Exercises

1. Create an image page that represents your finances. You can either use poster board or just a sheet of paper.

2. Cut pictures and words out of some of your favorite magazines. Find colorful pictures and whimsical symbols that reflect your positive financial transformation.

3. When finished, put it somewhere where you will see it often. I hope it makes you smile!

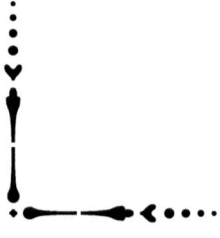

Step Six
Mastering Self Talk

You should be very proud and happy. The amount of progress you have made by working the first five steps to financial freedom is truly amazing. Give credit where credit is due. Congratulate yourself! Literally! Tell yourself right now that you have done a great job.

Think about it: Only a short time ago you wore the useless and self-defeating mindset of a victim. You let bad breaks and the decisions of other people control you. But you have admitted to yourself that your passive mindset just isn't working. You have summoned the energy and resolution necessary to change the way you look at your life and finances. And you have acted upon the revelations you have experienced, formulating and solidifying a powerful new set of goals. You have created a solid, workable *plan* that will enable you to manifest a whole new life, a self-empowered life where you now call the shots and decide when you will make things happen.

It's now time to work with your "self

talk," the voices in your head that form such a huge portion of your thoughts. In particular, you will begin to work with the voices that speak from your ego side – from your scared child and bully. When you rely on the decisions made by your ego, financial sabotage can easily result by hopping onto the poverty cycle without being conscious of it. What is so baffling is that the bully can masterfully give you the illusion that you are on the prosperity cycle.

POVERTY CYCLE

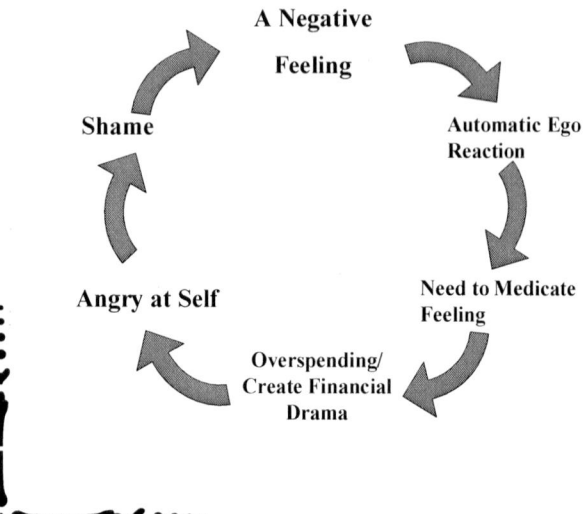

These ego voices distract you from experiencing the real you. They seem always on the verge of something dramatic and convincing. After all, the more frightened the scared child is, the more puffed up, aggressive and grandiose the bully becomes. When unchecked they can easily talk you into financial sabotage. They are not loving or nurturing. Rather, they are fearful, confused and have powerful destructive effects upon your consciousness and finances.

These thoughts, however, are just that: Thoughts. They are not "reality." And, because they are but thoughts, they can be categorized and identified. Here are the main categories of the negative thoughts that you will observe running through your head once you start paying attention

"*I can't*" thoughts.

These are perhaps the most prevalent of all negative thought forms especially with regards to your finances. The word "can't" is very possibly the most destructive word in the entire English language. Henry Ford once said, "Once you say, 'I can't,' whether it's right or wrong, it's true." Learn to say, "I can…", "I will…" Even if you don't feel like it at the time, encouraging yourself is making a decision not to give up.

"I shouldn't" thoughts.

These are a bit less frequent and are somewhat subtler. They often use our good boundaries against us by enforcing them at the wrong time in response to fear. Boundaries have their place. But if they lead us to action based on worry, anxiety and doubt, we're most likely operating in scared child or bully mode, rather than in the confidence of our wonder child and co-creator.

"Someone else thinks I can't" thoughts.

So often, a person will break out of victim consciousness and begin to make decisions, plans and positive goals, but the people around them will not be able to go to that place of freedom with them. They then make the big mistake of trying share their revelations with family and friends: "Hey, mom. I've decided that I'm just not going to be poor anymore. I'm not going to accept this anymore. I'm going to be a completely new person. Look at these great plans that I've made. I'm going to get a new job. I'm going to go ahead and proceed with my real estate venture I've told you about before. But this time, I'm really going to do it." And how does mom respond? "Oh honey, that's nice. Do you really think that's going to work? You know perfectly well that so and so tried that and failed completely. You have no training for any of this. I don't want to see you get hurt. You have to be realistic: There is no way that any of this is going to succeed. Honey, you're living in a dream world. It would be much better if you just accepted things as they are."

Mom, dad, brother, sister, best friend or co-worker is not going to be able to go with you right away to the new place of freedom, decisiveness, prosperity and abundance that you are creating. All they can see is what you have already done. You are the one who is breaking free, not them. Right now you are excited about the new life of financial freedom that you are creating for yourself. It's only natural that you want to share that with them. But doing so is actually a big mistake. Sharing is a matter of timing.

The time will come when you have actually worked the program that you have laid out for yourself. The time will come when it will be appropriate and correct for you to share. But your new discoveries are still a bit tenuous and fragile. Right now, the very best thing that you can do is to keep your plans to yourself.

"Someone else thinks I shouldn't" thoughts.

A large percentage of our most destructive self-talk actually derives from thoughts planted in our minds by other people. The thoughts behind this kind of self-talk can be hard to identify because they reach to our very deepest belief systems, our very selves. We typically look to other people, our peers, for validation of the way we act. We want to rely on feedback.

Parents play a huge part in this, despite their well-meant intentions. How many of us heard, at a very early age, things like "money is the root of all evil?" Or maybe we learned some variation on the theme that one of evil's most effective temptations is material wealth? Even those of us who may not have been reared in a home that directly taught such things have nonetheless been immersed in a mix of belief systems that carry all sorts of negative ideas about money and material wealth.

The first thing that must be done to deal with thoughts that fall into this category is to make an inventory of them. Write out all of the negative ideas and morals that other people and institutions have planted in your mind. Don't filter what comes out. Just write them down. Second, go over your list with one or more other people. Sometimes other people can readily identify ways of thinking that are hidden to us.

Once you have completed your list, look it over. What do you see? You may very well be passively and blindly accepting something you don't believe as "reality." Before you even think about trying to neutralize these very powerful and deeply embedded thoughts and ideas, it is very important that you realize and recognize the difficulty of your task. Living in denial won't help you one bit. You need to have your guard up with these thoughts if you are to summon the personal will necessary to get rid of them.

As was the case with other kinds of undesirable thoughts, trying to simply stop them in some way won't work. Replacing them with actual truth is a much better strategy. Search out the actual facts behind what you've been taught. You may be surprised to find some of the quotes you've heard don't exist in the form you thought.

It is entirely possible that doing this on your own won't work very well. If you've been living this long with these thoughts embedded in your mind and subconscious, you probably need someone else to help you get them out. You may even need to find a help group, join a different church or get involved in some sort of religion.

Fortunately there are a number of religious persuasions that are perfectly suited for this task. Having the terrific support of such a religion, via ministers, teachers, and friends within a congregation, books, CDs and so forth can be an absolutely spectacular addition to your life right about now. Even if you don't have a particularly large number of negative thought forms remaining from religious systems, your family or cultural forces, enlisting the help of a well-established group would promote the kind of healthy and thoroughly positive mindset that is crucial to the success of your financial healing.

"I don't deserve it" thoughts.

These thoughts stem from a poor self-image that is often the end result of all the previously listed negative thoughts. I haven't done enough work. I'm not a good enough person. I have done this or that terrible or borderline thing and therefore God can't really be behind me. These kinds of thoughts are easy to recognize and reject when they are in front of us. It's just that most of the time we don't recognize how little we value ourselves.

Take heart! These voices are not as powerful as you might think. You can reframe this negative self-talk to support you, empower you, and even make you wealthy! It is time to use the most powerful and valuable weapon you have – love.

Care for and nurture yourself. You have love inside of you, and it's possibly the strongest force within you. You emerged from the womb with it. It's a big part of you and probably the best part of you. Be easy and gentle on yourself. Jules

Renard so eloquently said, "Love is like an hourglass, with the heart filling up as the brain empties." Negative voices will try to convince you that you are actually weak, spineless and deserve some punishment for being so financially negligent and stupid. They're wrong and so far from the truth. If you feel this way, it is actually a positive sign that you're changing!!

We all have these internal voices – some stronger and louder than others. They come from the same characters. Let's just remove the mystery about them. They are a part of you, a very real part, but they are also very controllable. They can even be replaced with the best of you – your identity – the true, authentic, loving you. Negative voices can feel so powerful and strong but are in reality an illusion and paper-thin. Your identity is always the best part of you. It is where your love is. It is where you will know, without a doubt, that your needs are and will always be taken care of. Breathe a sigh of relief.

Here is an exercise I'd like you to try, just to see what comes up. Get a dollar bill (or a $5, $10, $50 or $100 …whatever you feel most comfortable with). Look at it. Feel it in your fingers. Now, if the dollar could talk, what would it say to you? Have your money write you a letter. Do not judge this exercise. Don't even think about it. Just do it.

If you feel daring enough and really want to be out of the box, so to speak, have your money write a letter to you from the different characters we discussed: from the scared child, the bully, the wonder child and co-creator. Put yourself in their shoes and feel their needs and wants. The sweet and touching part is usually what the wonder child and co-creator have to say. Can you see the different parts of you coming out? Which one do you want to engage? Learn to think like the wonder child and co-creator, and you'll be amazed at the results.

Give your ego a voice. We all have these characters – the scared child and bully. Ultimately, you can't ignore them or pretend they don't exist or aren't a part of you. So give them a voice. Let them be heard and say thank you. Then consciously choose your identity. It's that simple.

If you're still having trouble getting out of negative self-talk here are some other exercises: Practice affirming other people and yourself for wise financial decisions. Create a money journal to keep track of your feelings and thoughts. Set up a meeting with your financial adviser to facilitate putting positive energy on your goals.

Experiment with deliberately giving even a little money away – I'm always surprised how even $1 given for the sake of being kind to someone frees me from my own worries and makes other people smile. Or how about this: Go to your bank and get a few $2 bills (yes, they are still in circulation). Give the $2 as tips. Look at the response you get from people you give them to. It's priceless *and* affirming. Abundance rocks!

Doing any of these exercises will bring you to an emotional place that supports prosperity and reduces or eliminates financial stress and anxiety. They're now available to you any time you hear the sounds of a scared child or bully trying to convince you that it's too hard or complicated or that you don't deserve your rightful prosperity. Now is the time to take a leap of faith and action. Learn how to love yourself. You're already doing better than you think.

Step Six -
Mastering Self Talk
Questions and Exercises

1. Start writing your money & financial thoughts in a blank journal and call it your Financial Journal.

2. Pay close attention to how you talk to yourself about money. Is it positive or negative? If negative, can you identify a pattern of your favorite things you say to yourself about money? If so, write them down. If positive, write them down too.

3. Start recording to your financial wins, big and small. You might be surprised how many financial wins you actually have that go unnoticed.

Step Seven
Discipline

The last step got you in touch with the emotional side of what happens in the money equation. Hopefully, we have given you some tools that work. If you still feel enormous fear, I want to be on the safe side and say, "Go back and repeat Step Six". This is not failure. It is a mature decision you should be proud of. It takes character to admit you're not ready and discipline to commit yourself to mastering a technique before you move on.

Frequently, financial failure and poor financial decisions result from not backing up and questioning the choices and decisions we make before it is too late. Plowing ahead when that little voice is screaming inside of you to slow down only results in regret. Even if you have to go back five times, do it!

Years ago, a colleague of mine, an absolutely brilliant CPA, sat for the CPA exam time and time again – seven times in total before he finally passed. I don't know how many times he questioned his academic decision as he went through the process. Taking the exam over and over only made him feel like a failure. He was a great accountant but a lousy test taker. Every single time he studied the same way – self-study.

I remember discussing this with him and suggesting he attend classes rather than study on his own. Although both ways of studying are very well known in our little accounting world, most people favor one strategy over another. That was fine as long as the way he chose worked. But it didn't. Part of financial maturity is the willingness to try a different approach in conjunction with the financial tools available. The definition of insanity is doing the same thing over and over again and expecting a different result. Financial discipline commits to a plan on a day-to-day basis, keeping its eye on the target. It constantly chooses to make decisions that move toward the goal, not away from it. Not only does it require discipline, it takes discernment to make good decisions. Having the ability to discern means reviewing the options and selecting the one that most closely aligns with the goal. Discipline then lets the other options go, no matter what, and sticks to the plan.

If your plan is to spend within a certain realistic budget, then your commitment to stick with it requires discipline. It actually goes deeper than that. You know the moment when you see something you really want to buy but have to let something else go in order to stay within the budget. You either buy it unconsciously or stop and think. If you stop and think, you will make a conscious, realistic decision in line with your commitment. If you do not stop and think, you will probably buy it anyway and wonder why later. Are you serious about your goal? Are you serious about your commitment? If you are, you have to discipline yourself to choose long-term rewards rather than immediate gratification. Now is the time to practice, practice, practice.

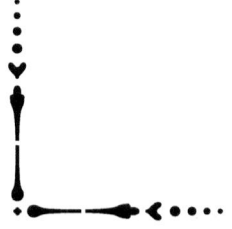

Step Seven - Discipline *Questions and Exercises*

1. Can you recall a recent financial transaction or experience in which you either felt regret or suffered consequences? If so, jot it in your Financial Journal.

2. See if you can pinpoint the moment you made the choice that later resulted in regret or a negative consequence.

3. Now write what you could or would have done differently to create a more desirable outcome.

4. Make a mental note to catch yourself earlier next time. You'll be surprised when you do!

Step Eight
Conscious Spending

Earlier we discussed the Ego/Identity Model and established that the Ego consisted of the scared child and bully. Most people deal with finances from their scared child. I base this on the multitude of clients I have consulted with over the years, and I'm sure these clients make up a representative sample of what is going on in the world at large.

It is important to know who controls your financial bus. If it is the scared child, money scares you, scarcity thinking dominates you, the future looks bleak and the whole financial "thing" is too complicated, what with taxes and all! You prefer to stay in financial denial and your pictures about money are based on lack. If any of this registers you are not alone. This thinking leads to unconscious spending, which is typically done by the bully.

The bully's role is to protect the scared child. When the scared child starts feeling horrible and afraid, the bully goes into action. It's very clever and can spend money like it is growing on trees with no regard to the future or sticking to a budget. Women are notorious for medicating their feelings by spending money. From their bully's point of view, they buy the new outfit in three different colors because it creates a sensation driven by adrenaline. This same illusion of wellness and vitality also runs rampant in men. They just usually buy different kinds of things.

I may be painting a rather hopeless picture. However, I am deliberately doing this to get your attention. If you can relate to this, it is a positive sign that you can distinguish between the characters in your head. Once you can identify these characters, you have free will to choose whom you will listen to.

In my own life, the part of me that is financially mature and wise is my co-creator. My co-creator's picture of money is based on abundance. She has the ability to create a financial plan and stick to it. She is realistic and does not sabotage my future by overspending for instant gratification. The co-creator in you can work with your financial advisor to establish a budget. Sticking to the budget requires the knowledge that gratification in the future is more important than gratification now. This does not take sacrifice. It takes maturity.

Conscious spending really means that you know what you are doing when you spend money. It means that you ask yourself questions like, "Is this purchase in any way going to jeopardize my financial plan?" or "Do I know what the financial parameters are ahead of time?" This sounds easy; but we often go "unconscious" in practice and our plan goes out the window. We'll deal with it later, we say. When later comes, we often have regret and shame and start the poverty cycle all over again.

Financial freedom largely depends upon mastering this step. I'm sure we can all look back and point to several examples in our lives when we could easily say, "If I had really stopped and thought about it, I would have taken a much different course of action".

The good news is that your life will offer many, many opportunities to stay conscious! Nothing creates a feeling of confidence and freedom more than the ability to stay awake when making decisions that have a positive impact on your life in the long run. When you spend money consciously, it makes the next step so much fun.

Step Eight - Conscious Spending Questions and Exercises

1. Recall a recent time when you had to make an important financial decision.

2. Write something simple an brief in your journal about the characters in your head (you know the ones...the committee) vying for attention.

3. Knowing what you know now, would you have made the same or a different decision? Which character in your head would you have listened to? Write it down.

Step Nine
Reward Yourself

If you have finally arrived here, you deserve not only to reward yourself, but to celebrate as well. You should always incorporate a consciously designed reward system into your plan for financial healing and recovery.

Recovery is great, but *it's only the beginning.* This is more than a method for stopping the debt and pain you have been experiencing. I want you to live in a state of superb fun, excitement, satisfaction, pleasure, delight, love, fun (did we say that already?), joy, supercharged health and vitality. Think bigger and then bigger again. Break through the completely imaginary boundaries and limitations you have unwittingly wrapped around you, so that you can really let go and reach heights that are amazing, beautiful, and an absolute...*blast!*

Modern psychologists, both behavioral and clinical, have intensively studied positive reinforcement for decades. It gets people to act. It's what really gets people to stop doing undesirable things and start doing things that are profitable, successful, productive, and healthy.

Negative reinforcement is also an effective way to get people to do things. If you yell at an employee, cut their pay, make them work nights or weekends, or give them unpleasant tasks, you can motivate them to change their behaviors. Striking an animal or giving it a jolt with a shock collar will stop them from doing an undesirable behavior right away. But any good animal trainer will tell you immediately that this type of negative training is far, far less effective than the positive reinforcement method. All of the very best animal trainers know that the way to really motivate an animal is to use systematic and highly pleasurable rewards.

So it is with you. Part of your brain includes an unbelievably complicated and extremely powerful system of automatic reflexes. This part of your brain, which neuroscientists commonly refer to as the autonomic nervous system is, for all practical purposes, a kind of animal brain. It reacts by avoiding negative stimuli and pursuing positive rewards. The negative reinforcement model will work, to some degree, but it's not necessary, or even acceptable. Now is the time to step up the evolutionary ladder and into the one hundred percent positive reinforcement system for self-improvement. Here are your assignments:

To begin with, it is a good idea to give yourself little rewards along the way. I know this goes against the grain of what many people say about making and meeting financial goals. For many advisors, financial success is usually achieved with sacrifice and hard work. Period. This is the reason so many people cannot manage to formulate a workable plan. Who wants to sacrifice? The whole "sacrifice" mindset might work for a while, but a plan that works for the long haul cannot be based on the unpleasant and painful framework of negative reinforcement.

Get out your time line. Look at the first few goals on it. A typical time line should contain things like, balance my checking account, negotiate with the IRS to reduce my penalties, refinance my mortgage or consolidate my Credit Card debt. Every item now needs to have a reward attached to it. So, from now on, when you are looking at your time line, you don't just see, "Renegotiate with the IRS." Instead you see,

Treat Myself to a One-Hour Massage With the Best Masseuse & Renegotiate my Penalties & Interest with the IRS.

Now substitute a different reward in the above sentence. Put something in there that is extremely pleasant or fun or exciting for *you*. It shouldn't be so expensive as to put you further into debt, but it should be nice enough, and generous enough to really make *you* feel like it is *well worth it* to call the IRS.

Using this dreaded call to the IRS as an example also helps illustrate another important point about the reward system for the time line, exchange value. Whenever you make a decision about a potential reward for any particular milestone or goal on your timeline, make sure you carefully consider and calculate the *real* value of your goal or milestone. In the case of a negotiation with the IRS, a typical person might end up saving several hundred or even several thousand dollars by simply having the presence of mind to *try* negotiating. Should that be the case, the reward should have a suitable exchange value and should not be too cheap or "tight."

Go through your time line and carefully consider the rewards that you assign to each item on the time line that you will achieve. Use your best handwriting and print the reward carefully right next to each milestone, with larger and bolder letters for the reward than for the goal itself. If you use this sincerely and in the right way, when you are done adding the rewards to your time line, the *life* ahead of you is actually a series of rewards.

Your life is a series of rewards.

That sounds good doesn't it? It's completely different than the defeatist, downtrodden, anxiety-laden, debt-ridden view of life you may have had when you started reading this book.

How does your time line of rewards really look now? How does your life look now? Did you put plenty of really fun stuff on there? Were you nice and generous to yourself? Did you put things on there that are a bit spectacular without being financially irresponsible?

Make your rewards more and more meaningful as you successfully take larger financial steps and get closer to or meet your financial goals. You deserve it! And, above all, *work with your financial advisor to make sure that your rewards make sense financially and work for you, and not against you.*

For example, let's say that one of your largest and most important goals is to pay all of your credit cards off completely--a goal that almost everyone should have. Let's say you and your financial advisor have determined that this is so important that it deserves a super-exciting and special reward: A Caribbean cruise! Normally a Caribbean cruise that will cost $3000 is the last thing that a person with several thousand dollars in credit card debt should be splurging on. The important thing is to realize just how important paying off your credit card debt really is. Normal interest rates for credit cards typically range from 17% to 20%. This means that when you pay off this debt, you actually pay a lot more than the amount that you *appear* to owe. Credit card companies design the minimum to get you to pay double or triple that amount. Getting rid of this kind of debt is therefore extremely important to your financial health. If it takes the promise of a Caribbean cruise, or a trip to Hawaii, or a large flat-screen plasma TV, or whatever your pleasure may be—so be it.

The trick is to pay the debt off while at the same time saving enough for the reward. Let's say you make a decision to pay off the credit cards over a 36-month period. Your advisor then shows you how to consolidate the credit card debts into one monthly payment. You incorporate the necessary monthly payment into your budget. However, in addition you figure out how much you have to save every month to end up with enough money at the end of the thirty-six months to pay for your reward.

If your cruise is going to cost $3000 then you "pay yourself" $83.33 per month ($83.33 * 36 months = $3000 rounded up). At the same time, you work with your advisor to stop racking up any more debt. If you stop using your credit cards in the way that you have been in the past, you will be saving a huge amount of money, easily equal to the $83.33 per month or far exceeding it. In the end, you will have paid off all the cards, paid for the trip, and saved a bundle on the fees and interest that would have accrued if you had not followed this relatively simple plan.

This is how you need to start thinking about your time line. When you start adding in the rewards, make sure that they will give you a life that is fun, happy and exciting. Your time line and your life will begin to take on a completely different color and a completely new excitement.

A number of fun things and fabulous ways to reward yourself are either inexpensive or free. When your financial goals become more important than instant gratification, it is incredible how resourceful and creative you can be! You will begin to look at your recovery not as a sacrifice of any kind but as a healthy replacement of activities!

Close your eyes and fast-forward your life five years. Think of the feeling you will get when you know without a doubt that you are on track to meet your financial goals, regardless of the time line you have chosen. Your life surely will be different just from knowing you can keep commitments with yourself! This is cause for a big celebration!

Step Nine - Reward Yourself Questions and Exercises

1. In your Journal, list five financial goals, big and small, on the left side of the paper.

2. Beside each financial goal, assign a reward that is equivalent to the size of the goal.

3. Assign a reward to YOURSELF today, yes today, right now, just for getting this far! You have my permission.

Step Ten
Review the Plan

As time goes by and you meet your financial goals, you will need to review your plan. New information will emerge, making the plan that you have been following obsolete or out of line with your goals. Your goals may even change. Your financial plan should become precious to you and will need nurturing and protection similar to a small child in your care. It's your responsibility to keep it healthy and watch it grow with you.

You should set aside time at least once a year to keep your plan dynamic and fluid. If you allow it to become stagnant, you will lose interest in it. A comfortable window exists on the continuum where one end is stagnation and the other end is obsession. As you practice sound financial principles that work for you, you should easily find this area of comfort.

When a plan fails, it is usually for one of two reasons. Either Step One doesn't happen or Step Ten doesn't happen. In other words, either a person does not want to wake up and take responsibility for their finances, or they have followed the steps but failed to review the plan. Not initiating either step usually leads to the poverty cycle. This is not meant to scare you, but to remind you to be prudent and realistic.

The law of perpetuation works in both directions. If you spend money compulsively you can accumulate massive debt quickly. But if you start saving money and creating wealth, it builds up quicker than you think and usually in a compounded way.

Take a savings account, for instance. The money you have in a savings account grows in three ways. The first is adding more money. The second is earning interest income on this money. The third is making interest income on the original money plus adding more money plus interest on the interest you have made. Whew…can you wrap your mind around that?

Let's look at it at a slightly different angle, step by step. You create a savings account by putting an initial amount of money in the bank. The bank then multiplies by a rate of interest and puts this money into your account as well. If you add a bit more money to your account, you now have the initial money you put in plus the interest income the bank put in plus the additional amount that you put in again. The bank's interest is then "compounded", meaning you make more interest on the interest the bank has already paid. If you started with $100 and the bank is paying 5% interest compounded annually, the first year you will make $5 in interest ($100 x 5% = $5.00). The second year you will make 5% on $105, or $5.25, resulting in a total of $110.25 at the end of the second year.

Now imagine you accumulate $1000, and it is compounded monthly instead of annually. You will make money on the money you have already made on a monthly basis. The interest you make (also called the return on your investment) is known as passive income because you do not have to do anything to earn this money. You even earn this money while you sleep and on weekends when you may be watching the game! When you work and receive a salary, this money is called earned income because you "do something" to earn it. When you have a savings or money market account, you don't have to do anything to earn the interest income - it's automatic. You actually meet your financial goals quicker than you thought because you perpetuate wealth instead of debt.

Reviewing your plan can be quite empowering, especially if you have already met your initial goals. If you have, you're past the toughest part. Congratulations! This means that you are indeed replacing old habits from the poverty cycle with new habits that keep you in the prosperity cycle. You will see the distance you have come and how much fun it becomes to create new financial goals knowing that you are most likely to succeed! Plus, it's always encouraging to work with more wealth (the strong foundation) rather than sort through a shame producing mess.

Reviewing the plan not only includes a review of the numbers and goals, it also includes an internal review as well. Take time to review what's going on inside of you, the health of your self-talk, wonder child and co-creator. You may have an excellent plan, but it's those parts that drive you to success. Make a serious review of which behaviors work, as well as which behaviors don't work, and make adjustments accordingly. Remember, we don't get to come into this lifetime without an ego. It won't disappear, I promise. I think the best we can do is stay awake, be aware, give the ego a voice, let it talk, let it feel bad because that is all it knows how to do. Then gently push it aside and consciously choose your identity. This would be the time to make an appointment with your advisor to discuss your plan and your thoughts about your experiences. Your advisor will be able to offer suggestions and lay out options just as she or he did in the beginning.

You have created a solid foundation. You have recognized and begun listening to the wonder child and co-creator inside you. Don't forget to continually discipline yourself to choose long-term financial prosperity over unconscious acts of self-sabotage. Abundance is our birthright. Everyone can experience it. It's time to start integrating what we've learned in our lives so we can start using money to love others and ourselves.

At the end of the preface to this book, I said "the key that will unlock the truth of my story and the financial healing you're about to experience is that *it all has to start with love."*

It also ends with love. Love is all there is. *Priceless…*

Step Ten - Review the Plan
Questions And Exercises

1. Pull out a calendar and mark two dates in the next 12 months, six months apart, to meet with your financial adviser.

2. Mark two separate dates, six months apart, to meet with YOURSELF and review your plan as well as your self talk.

3. Look back and write, as honestly as possible, what is and is not working in your financial life. Adjust accordingly.

4. Now look in the mirror, into your eyes and say these words, "Congratulations, your future looks prosperous. I love you and I will take care of you!!" If you feel silly doing this, do it again!

Bibliography/References

1. Desjardins Unified Model of Treatment has many components. The Ego-Identity (scared child, bully, etc.) is a small component of the Model. The Desjardins are currently involved with HIGHER POWER PRODUCTIONS in Austin, Texas where they do workshops and are concentrating their efforts on helping individuals identify and process the deep seated self limiting belief systems.
www.higherpower.info
The entire Desjardins Unified Model of Treatment is designed as a closed model for inpatient Treatment. The Desjardins originated the model in Canada. The value and uniqueness is in the sequencing of therapeutic approaches possible only in a closed inpatient program that promotes therapeutic alliances. For further information on the inpatient program contact: Liliane Desjardins at liliane@higherpower.info.

2. Although Deepak Chopra popularized this quantum physics theory in his book "Quantum Healing", Hugh Everett III, in 1957, originally proposed this radical new way of dealing with some of the more perplexing aspects of quantum mechanics and it forever became known as the "Many-Worlds Interpretation" as well as "The Everett Interpretation."

3   Quicken is a popular computer software manufactured by Intuit, Inc. to easily track and manage your personal finances and assets. This product interfaces with online banking.

4   According to Robert McCrum, William Cran & Robert MacNeil in The Story of English, New York: Penguin, 1992:1 there are approximately 1,000,000 words in the English language (including scientific words)
    "Time" is #68 on "The First 100 Most Commonly Used English Words" from "The Reading Teachers Book of Lists", Third Edition, by Edward Bernard Fry, Ph.D, Jacqueline E. Kress, Ed.D. & Dona Lee Fountoukidis, Ed.D.
    According to the 100-million-word "British National Corpus", the word "time" is #53 as the most frequently used words in English.

5   "Money is the root of all evil" is a common figure of speech signifying that money causes serious problems and people would be better off without it. This quote is #14 on the Wikipedia Encyclopedia's List of Famous Misquotations. It is the most misquoted and misinterpreted verse in the Bible. The correct quote, according to Apostle Paul in 1 Timothy 6:10, is "For the love of money is the root of all evil: which while some coveted after, they have erred from the faith, and pierced themselves through with many sorrows" (King James Version). The Amplifying Bible's says "For the love of money (and all it buys) placed before the love of God (in reality) is the root of all kinds of evil." There is a clear distinction

between "the love of" or worship of money versus money itself being the root of all evil.

6   Skinner, B.F., 1953, Science and Human Behavior, New York: Macmillan
    Skinner, B.F., 1969, Contingencies of Reinforcement: A Theoretical Analysis, New York: Appleton-Century-Crofts
    Walker, S, 1975, Learning and Reinforcement, Mathuen & Co Ltd
    Mazur J.E., 1986, Learning and Behavior (Third Edition), Prentice Hall

7   According to the American Heart Association, the ***autonomic nervous system*** (ANS) is a regulatory structure that helps people adapt to changes in their environment. It adjusts or modifies some functions in response to stress.

8   According to the triune ('tri' as in 3 part) brain theory developed by Dr. Paul MacLean, Chief of Brain Evolution and Behavior at the National Institutes of Health, you have three brains, not just one. This theory helps explain some of your behaviors (and those of others!). The R-complex or brainstem is the ***reptilian brain*** and lies in between the other two parts (the Limbic system and the neo-cortex). The reptilian brain is a remnant of our prehistoric past. It acts on stimulus and response and is useful for quick decisions without thinking. It focuses on survival and takes over when you are in danger and don't have time to think.

What is Wizard Academy?

Composed of a fascinating series of workshops led by some of the most accomplished instructors in America, Wizard Academy is a progressive new kind of business and communications school whose stated objective is to improve the creative thinking and communication skills of sales professionals, internet professionals, business owners, educators, ad writers, ministers, authors, inventors, journalists and CEOs.

Founded in 1999, the Academy has exploded into a worldwide phenomenon with an impressive fraternity of alumni who are rapidly forming an important worldwide network of business relationships.

"Alice in Wonderland on steroids! I wish Roy Williams had been my very first college professor. If he had been, everything I learned after that would have made a lot more sense and been a lot more useful... Astounding stuff."
—Dr. Larry McCleary,
Neurologist and Theoretical Physicist

"...Valuable, helpful, insightful, and thought provoking. We're recommending it to everyone we see."
—Jan Nations and Sterling Tarrant
senior managers, Focus on the Family

"Be prepared to take a wild, three-ring-circus journey into the creative recesses of the brain... [that] will change your approach to managing and marketing your business forever. For anyone who must think critically or write creatively on the job, the Wizard Academy is a must."

—Dr. Kevin Ryan
Pres., The Executive Writer

"Even with all I knew, I was not fully prepared for the experience I had at the Academy… Who else but a wizard can make sense of so many divergent ideas? I highly recommend it."

—Mark Huffman,
Advertising Production Manager,
Procter & Gamble

"A life-altering 72 hours."

—Jim Rubart

To learn more about Wizard Academy, visit www.WizardAcademy.org or call the academy at (800) 425-4769